DEAR BRUCE,

TOGETHER WE ⟨✓ P9-DHN-608⟩ ...ER

TOGETHER WE CAN SUCCESSFULLY

REACH THE OTHER SIDE, AND

TOGETHER WE ARE NOT ALONE.

IN THIS CHALLENGING MOMENT

OF DISRUPTIVE CHANGE, IT IS

IMPORTANT TO FOCUS ON THE

BASICS AND LEAVE FEAR

BEHIND. THIS EASY READ OF

BUSINESS COMMANDMENTS OFFERS

A THOUGHT PROVOKING FORMULA

THANK YOU FOR EVERYTHING

YOU DO TO MAKE HEARTS

ON FIRE GREAT.

LOVE,

GLENN

# The Ten Commandments for Business Failure

# DONALD R. KEOUGH

# The
# Ten Commandments
# for Business
# Failure

Portfolio

PORTFOLIO
Published by the Penguin Group
Penguin Group (USA) Inc., 375 Hudson Street,
New York, New York 10014, U.S.A.
Penguin Group (Canada), 90 Eglinton Avenue East, Suite 700, Toronto,
Ontario, Canada M4P 2Y3 (a division of Pearson Penguin Canada Inc.)
Penguin Books Ltd, 80 Strand, London WC2R 0RL, England
Penguin Ireland, 25 St. Stephen's Green, Dublin 2, Ireland
(a division of Penguin Books Ltd)
Penguin Books Australia Ltd, 250 Camberwell Road, Camberwell,
Victoria 3124, Australia (a division of Pearson Australia Group Pty Ltd)
Penguin Books India Pvt Ltd, 11 Community Centre,
Panchsheel Park, New Delhi–110 017, India
Penguin Group (NZ), 67 Apollo Drive, Rosedale, North Shore 0632,
New Zealand (a division of Pearson New Zealand Ltd)
Penguin Books (South Africa) (Pty) Ltd, 24 Sturdee Avenue,
Rosebank, Johannesburg 2196, South Africa

Penguin Books Ltd, Registered Offices: 80 Strand, London WC2R 0RL, England

First published in 2008 by Portfolio, a member of Penguin Group (USA) Inc.

1 3 5 7 9 10 8 6 4 2

Grateful acknowledgment is made for permission to reprint the following copyrighted works:
Excerpt from "Sell the Mailroom" by Peter Drucker. Originally published in *The Wall Street Journal*, July 25, 1989. Reprinted with permission.
Pepsi jingle. Pepsi-Cola is a registered trademark of PepsiCo, Inc. Used with permission.

LIBRARY OF CONGRESS CATALOGING IN PUBLICATION DATA
Keough, Donald R.
The ten commandments for business failure / Donald R. Keough.
p. cm.
ISBN 978-1-59184-234-7
1. Business failures. I. Title. II. Title: 10 commandments for business failure.
HG3761.K46 2008
658—dc22      2008017767

Printed in the United States of America    Set in Janson Text

*This book is dedicated to
the millions of men and women
past, present, and future who make up the
remarkable Coca-Cola family
around the world.*

# Contents

Foreword by Warren Buffett     ix

Introduction     1

Commandment One—Top of the List:
**Quit Taking Risks**     11

Commandment Two:
**Be Inflexible**     25

Commandment Three:
**Isolate Yourself**     45

Commandment Four:
**Assume Infallibility**     59

Commandment Five:
**Play the Game Close to the Foul Line**     67

Commandment Six:
**Don't Take Time to Think**     81

Commandment Seven:

**Put All Your Faith in Experts and Outside Consultants**    97

Commandment Eight:

**Love Your Bureaucracy**    115

Commandment Nine:

**Send Mixed Messages**    133

Commandment Ten:

**Be Afraid of the Future**    151

Commandment Eleven:

**Lose Your Passion for Work—for Life**    173

Acknowledgments    187

# Foreword

IT HAS BEEN AN ARTICLE of faith for me that I should always try to hang out with people who are better than I. There is no question that by doing so you move yourself up. It worked for me in marriage and it's worked for me with Don Keough.

When I'm with Don Keough, I can feel myself on the up escalator. He has an optimistic view of me and what I am to the extent that he raises my sights and makes me believe more in myself and the world around me. When you are around Don, you are learning something all the time. He's an incredible business leader. The greatest achievement of good executives is to get things done through other people, not themselves. Now here is a guy who is capable of getting all kinds of people from all over the world, men and women who want to help him succeed. I've seen him do it.

Maybe it is because no one understands the human aspects of situations better than he. He can advise my kids perhaps better than I can and they love him for that. He does the same for everyone he calls a friend—and that is a lot of people.

The Graham Group, named after my mentor Ben Graham, is a bunch of people who meet every two years or so. All my close friends, including Don, attend. Everyone wants Don to be the keynote speaker. Bill Gates, in particular, always wants it to be Don Keough. He just loves listening to him because Don talks such sense and offers such inspiration. Don can tell you to go to hell so wonderfully you'll enjoy the journey.

He is on my board at Berkshire Hathaway because he is one of the very few guys I feel I can hand the keys over to.

We go back almost fifty years together, to the time we lived opposite each other on Farnam Street here in Omaha. We were just two guys making a living for our families back then. If we had told you that one of us would become president of The Coca-Cola Company and the other would become head of Berkshire Hathaway, I'm sure you would have said I hope their parents have enough money to support these two.

At one point I knocked on his door and asked him to invest ten thousand dollars or so with me. He turned me down flat. I'd probably have turned me down too back then.

Our families were great friends; the kids were always

in and out of each other's houses. It was very tough on my kids when they had to move to Houston. There were a lot of tears that day when they moved away.

It's interesting when you think of it. Don and I were living less than a hundred yards away from where my future partner, Charlie Munger, had grown up. Don went to Houston and Atlanta; Charlie landed in Los Angeles. But we later reunited as close friends and business associates, all with a lot of Omaha still in us. Nowadays, of course, a lot of people say they are from Omaha for status reasons!

After Don left Omaha we kept in touch over the years. I'd meet him at the Alfalfa Club or once we even met at the White House. Then he read an article in 1984 in which I praised Pepsi, "preferably with a touch of cherry syrup in it." The next day he sent me their new product, Cherry Coke, and invited me to taste test "the nectar of the Gods." After I drank it I told him, "Forget about your testing. I don't know much about that stuff but I do know this is a winner."

I switched brands right away and immediately declared Cherry Coke the official soft drink of Berkshire Hathaway.

A few years later I started buying Coke stock but I didn't tell Don because I felt he might have to tell the company lawyer, and who knows where that would have led. I didn't want to put him in an awkward position.

Anyway, he called and said, "You wouldn't happen to be buying a share or two of Coke stock, now would you?" I told him, "It so happens that I am." At the time we picked up 7.7 percent of the company.

It was a straightforward decision, especially knowing that he was the president. I saw Coke in 1988 as a company that understood what it was doing and was doing the right thing and was obviously enormously valuable as a result.

If you wanted to invent a human personification of The Coca-Cola Company, it would be Don Keough. He was and is Mr. Coke. He's of the Ben Franklin school, "Keep thy shop and it will keep thee." Basically, what he has always done is do the right thing by Coca-Cola and he believes that it will always do the right thing by him.

Don's best ability is to cut to the chase on an issue, to cut through the bureaucratic fog. Keep it simple is his principle and mine too.

Herbert Allen says that the only two businessmen he knew who could have become president if they had run for office were Jack Welch and Don Keough. I agree with that; they both had that natural brilliance. They are both people we can learn so much from.

After all these years, every time I see Don Keough I feel as refreshed as I do after drinking a Cherry Coke. He never loses his carbonation. I've seen him on the board of Coke and now at Berkshire. Don is as enthusiastic and committed as ever, full of plans, energy, ideas, daring us all to dream. I am delighted that this book will help so many other people share in that unique Keough vision.

—Warren Buffett

# The
# Ten Commandments
# for Business
# Failure

# Introduction

MORE THAN TWO DECADES ago as president of The Coca-Cola Company, I was invited to be the keynote speaker at a large convention of customers meeting in Miami. The theme of their meeting was "Join the Winners," and they asked if I would speak to them on how to be a winner in business. In short, they asked for the secrets of success.

It was a flattering assignment, but there has never been a shortage of speakers and writers willing to dispense tried and true advice on how to succeed in business without really trying. From football coaches to ex-CEOs to psychologists to teachers, preachers, and fortune-tellers, the success gurus have paraded their wares across the pages and stages of the world. And while there is some good in everything, most of those efforts boiled down to the easy bromides of "Work hard" and "Do what your mother tells you." After a lifetime in business, I've never been able to develop a set of rules or a step-by-step formula that will guarantee success in anything, much less in a field as dynamic and changing as business.

Take the whole question of leadership, which has been studied to death, always inconclusively. A sociology professor who had spent his entire academic life studying leadership once said that he had followed the careers of nearly two thousand students who had gone through his classes, and after all this research he had arrived at the conclusion that the only way to identify a leader is to look behind the person to see if anybody is following him or her.

So when I was asked to talk about how to win, my response was I couldn't do that. What I could do, however, was to talk about how to lose and I offered a guarantee that anyone who followed my formula would be a highly successful loser.

So I delivered a little speech that has been refined over time into "Keough's Ten Commandments for Business Failure" and which evolved over more time into this little book, which draws on more than sixty years of experience, beginning in 1949 with the then-new medium of television at WOW-TV in Omaha, Nebraska.

I had my first taste of television while attending Creighton University on the GI bill after service in the navy in World War II. With some hazy idea of maybe going on to law school, I got a degree in the humanities, majoring in philosophy. Over the years, however, I've never seen a help-wanted ad for a philosopher. I enjoyed studying the great debates over man and his place in the universe, the nature of good and evil, the shadows and realities of life. While MBA graduates scoff at such "useless" knowledge, most of our known world history can be attributed to the realization or clashing of ideas spun out years earlier by some long-dead philosophers.

My humanities interests in college also took me into the debating society, extemporaneous speaking, and eventually the performing arts, where I was "discovered" and asked to host a live closed-circuit event at the university medical school. The live event was an operation being performed on a sick animal, beamed over the circuit to TV sets in the large lecture theater. Unfortunately, it was not live for very long because the poor animal died early in the procedure, leaving me with a lot of empty airtime to fill until another animal was brought in. Thank God, it was only closed-circuit television and there were probably only a few people in the hall. Frankly, I think it made me a pioneer in "reality" TV. Even though hooked on communications, I took some law courses and gave the law a chance to captivate me. Ultimately, however, I returned to communications.

While in school, I received a media scholarship, which gave me the opportunity to become an intern at WOW-TV. As luck would have it, my first assignment was to be the play-by-play announcer on the first-ever TV transmission of a live professional football game west of Chicago. It was a National Football League preseason game between the Los Angeles Rams and the New York Giants being played in Omaha. The usual sports announcer had taken one look at the newfangled medium and passed on the assignment while remarking to anyone who would listen that televising sports events would never work.

The Rams-Giants game was not the highlight of my life. The field was a converted baseball stadium and the broadcast booth was high behind home plate, which put me in front of a microphone in the deepest reaches of the end zone. The stadium was poorly lit, I could see only half the field, and my spotter, who was to help me identify the players, showed up drunk. I was less than articulate. At one point I said, "The ball is on the one-inch line."

The coverage of the game was a prelude to WOW's live telecasting of the University of Nebraska's home games later that year. The common mantra is that Husker football is the state religion. There were only a few hundred television sets in all of Nebraska at the time but that did nothing to diminish the enthusiasm of the management of the station, who saw and believed, presciently, that the new medium would soon sweep all before it. Ultimately, it did.

After my inauspicious beginning with the Rams-Giants game, however, I was allowed to go on to cover all the Nebraska games that year. I had to help lug all of the equipment up to the tiny broadcast booth, but it was worth it. I was rewarded with the princely sum of fifty-five dollars a week. For that salary I also did a daily talk show called *Keough's Coffee Counter*, which was directly followed by a much more professional and funnier program hosted by another young man starting out in the new medium, Johnny Carson. He also made fifty-five dollars a week. Johnny and I became lifelong friends.

While the broadcasting business was interesting, the sponsor of my talk show, Paxton and Gallagher's Butternut Coffee, offered the more generous sum of seventy-five dollars a week to join their company. Paxton and Gallagher was a regional food wholesaler headquartered in Omaha. The new job meant a bit more money, less time traveling, and more time at home with my new wife, Mickie, so I made the jump into the corporate world in late 1950 and never looked back.

In 1958, Gilbert and Clarke Swanson, fresh from the sale of their hugely successful Swanson Foods to Campbell Soups, bought Paxton and Gallagher from the Gallagher family. They renamed it Butternut Foods and had great expansion plans. So I entered a new chapter in my business life. The Swanson brothers, by the way, had made their initial fortune in the 1950s on an extremely simple product with new freezing technology that combined two consumer desires of the time—the desire to watch more television and the desire for more convenient cooking and the TV dinner came into existence.

After the death of Clarke Swanson, Butternut Foods

was sold and I found myself with a new job in a new and larger company, Duncan Foods in Houston, Texas. The company was headed by Charles Duncan, who later became president of The Coca-Cola Company and subsequently served as deputy secretary of defense and secretary of energy in the Carter administration.

Subsequently Duncan Foods was acquired by The Coca-Cola Company, where I then went on through a series of roles helping to represent the world's best-known brand for more than thirty years, ending up following Duncan as president in 1981. The bulk of my entire business career has been within The Coca-Cola Company, so you will find quite a number of references to life in that remarkable global organization.

There is a certain justification for using The Coca-Cola Company examples because the enterprise is so varied and multidimensional. It involves everything from manufacturing to distribution to retailing, from street vendors to big box outlets, and touches so many different people of all races, religions, and cultures in nearly two hundred countries. With The Coca-Cola Company, I met presidents, dictators, captains of industry, poets, painters, and movie stars. More important, I had the privilege of talking with Coca-Cola bottler partners, retail food store customers and consumers in every corner of the globe from the Arctic Circle to the southernmost tip of Tierra del Fuego, from mainland

China to anarchic corners of sub-Saharan Africa. While no company can ever embrace all of the world and all of mankind, Coca-Cola comes about as close as any.

Throughout this book when I note instances of company executives, including me, falling into one or more of the failure traps, I am pleased to also point out that most failures were relatively short-lived, corrective measures were taken quickly, and the company survived and prospered. In 2008 it is in a new growth period under the leadership of Neville Isdell, who is concluding his remarkable run as chief executive officer, and CEO-elect Muhtar Kent, a brilliant individual who has a deep respect for the Coca-Cola system and its people.

At the outset, it is important to explain the relationship between Roberto Goizueta and me during our twelve years in leadership together at The Coca-Cola Company. While we had both worked for the company for years and were friends, in early March of 1981, Roberto became the chairman and CEO and I the president and chief operating officer.

We had a unique and close relationship and a big job in front of us. Roberto gave me as COO and a fellow director broad authority to energize the Coca-Cola system in more than two hundred countries around the world. Make no mistake about it though, while he was generous in delegating authority to me, he could not and did not delegate his ultimate responsibility as the

CEO. He was in fact my boss and one of the most brilliant leaders in American business history. In 1981, the market value of the company was $4 billion and when he died in 1997 it was $145 billion.

Since retiring from The Coca-Cola Company more than a decade ago, I have remained active in the business world as chairman of Allen & Company, the investment banking firm. So with that background, I give you these ten commandments and with them comes the assurance that if you carefully follow one or more you will fail, or at least have a head start on the downward path to ultimate failure. Believe me there's no shortage of failure. According to the U.S. bankruptcy courts, 20,152 businesses declared bankruptcy in the first three quarters of 2007.

There is an army of self-declared business experts who can explain why this happened. They are armed with thousands of PowerPoint slides providing elaborate strategic explanations for failure . . . poor customer service, underestimating competition, supply chain disconnects, bad acquisitions, and/or too much debt. These are usually described as an abstract collective failure— "The company failed to innovate. The company ignored the founders. The company did this. The company did not do that."

But companies are artificial constructs. A company doesn't fail to do anything. Individuals do, and when you probe a bit you usually find that failure lies not in a litany of strategic mistakes—though they all may be present in one form or another—but the real fault lies, as Shakespeare noted, in ourselves, the leaders of the business. Businesses are the product and extension of the personal characteristics of its leaders—the lengthened shadows of the men and women who run them. They are the main actors on the business stage and when, through one or more personal failings, they take a business in the wrong direction, then the business is headed for failure.

While these commandments can be applied to any business at any stage in its development, they are mainly intended for businesses and business leaders who have already attained a measure of success. In fact, the more you have achieved, the more these commandments apply to you. If you are the leader of an enterprise, large or small, that is achieving great sales and profits, be careful. That is the time you are in danger of grasping one of my commandments and failure is just around the corner.

These rules for failure are certainly not an indictment of anyone in particular, though some individuals are mentioned as examples. Nor are the commandments startling breakthroughs in management thinking. They just make common sense.

Show me a failed business, even one based on the latest wikinomics, and I will bet you with considerable assurance that their leaders have violated more than one

of these commandments. One step toward failure, un-
checked, leads to another.

So view this little book as a cautionary tale. If you
find yourself a disciple of one or more of these commandments, watch out. You are on your way to failure
and taking your company with you.

# Commandment One—Top of the List

## Quit Taking Risks

> *"He that is overcautious will accomplish little."*
> —Friedrich von Schiller

FOR MOST OF MANKIND FOR most of history risk aversion was the prevailing mood. Hunters and gatherers wandered far and wide, we presume, but after the agricultural revolution allowed people to settle down, most of them did so. People chose to live as their fathers and mothers and their grandfathers and grandmothers before them had lived, never venturing far from the village. And with good reason. It was a dangerous world out there. Just look at the old maritime maps with their ominous areas labeled "terra incognito"—territory unknown—sometimes embellished with even more threatening warnings, such as "Here be dragons." Who would want to take a risk sailing into such places?

A few did, of course. But most people stayed home. Many things could happen to you if you took a risk, and most of them were probably bad.

Even today, much of the world in sub-Saharan

Africa, parts of the Middle East, and parts of Southeast Asia is still mired in a risk-averse "Let's-do-it-like-we-always-did-it-because-that's-the-way-we-always-did-it" culture. The cycle of sameness is unbroken from generation unto generation, often in families and groups living in the deepest poverty.

America, on the other hand, has been from the very beginning about risk taking. From Columbus to Jamestown to the Second Continental Congress and Thomas Jefferson's eloquent Declaration of Independence, this nation has been built on one risk after another. We are the descendants of tough, resilient risk takers who put everything, including their lives, on the line and survived almost insurmountable odds. Hector St. John de Crevecoeur wrote in 1782, "Here individuals of all nations are melted into a new race of men whose labours and posterity will one day cause great changes in the world. . . . The American is a new man."

My own great grandfather Michael Keough was only eighteen in 1848 when he left Ireland and all alone took the risk to cross the "bitter bowl of tears," as the Atlantic was called. Conditions on the ships were ghastly, with overcrowding, rats, filth, disease, and hard-bitten captains who cared little for their cargo. En route, bodies were tossed overboard or off-loaded at the first landfall. On the island of Grosse Île in Canada, thousands of Irish immigrants are buried in unmarked graves. Only the African slaves reached the United States in worse shape.

Those immigrants who did make it discovered that what awaited them was seldom the Promised Land, but a future of brutal dawn-to-dark work. My great grandfather found the only job he could get was lifting stone in a Pittsfield, Massachusetts, quarry, sixteen hours a day, one step above prison work. Nevertheless, this hard labor provided a little food and security and, because he soon married and had children, it's reasonable to think that Michael might have been tempted to settle down and stay in Pittsfield.

It's reasonable to think that because when you achieve something, even very little, there is the great temptation to quit taking risks.

It's human nature. I've got something. Why risk it? Who knows what's on the other side of the mountain? Don't go there!

I imagine my great grandfather heard such voices in his head and probably from some of the people around him in Pittsfield.

"Stay here. You've got a job. Lifting rocks is an honorable occupation. There are thousands out there who have nothing!"

But instead of settling into the known, albeit backbreaking, routine Pittsfield offered, Michael took a risk and migrated across half the continent in an oxen-drawn prairie schooner to a far-off land called Iowa. I'm glad he did.

His son, John, my grandfather, continued to expand the Iowa homestead, risking everything, year after year on crops that were subject to blizzards, dust storms, and grasshoppers. I remember being told that because there were so few trees on the property, grandfather had to drive a team of horses about twenty miles once a week to the Rock River, where he would cut wood, the only source of fuel. One day, he swung the ax and cut off his toe. He simply shoved the toe back on, bound it up with burlap, and finished his work.

The toe, the foot, and my grandfather survived— without antibiotics, I might add.

We in this country have a unique gene pool. Most of us come from a long line of remarkable individuals who boarded the boat when most other people stayed behind. Many didn't even get a chance to get to shore. And those who did survive the journey across the Atlantic or the Pacific (or the mountains or the prairies or the desert) were then rewarded with season after season of unbelievable hardship on farms or in building railroads or in dangerous and dirty mines and factories unimaginable today. In 1900, American families spent nearly twice as much on funerals as they did on medicine. Somehow they prevailed.

Against a background of overcoming challenges like

those our ancestors overcame makes a day, any day, at the office a walk in the park.

Yet as our lives get softer and richer and more comfortable, the temptation to quit taking risks is so great.

It's one of the major diseases of success. It's easy to succumb, particularly as you get older. I don't mean age sixty. This disease can strike at age forty. You say to yourself, "I've been out on a limb all my life . . . worrying, losing sleep. Let somebody else do that now. I'm content with the status quo."

Some might conclude that the risk taken by the start-up entrepreneur who mortgages his house and everything else in order to try a new idea or even pioneer a whole new industry is the most difficult kind of risk to take. Four out of five new businesses fail. Most new products never make it out of the test market, and if they do they have only a one in thirteen chance of success. The National Federation of Independent Business Research Foundation estimates that after just five years only half of new businesses with employees are still operating, and many of those at a loss. It certainly isn't easy.

But equally difficult, and sometimes more so, is to undertake a risk from a position of substantial ongoing success—to undertake a risk when there is considerable evidence that it might not even be necessary. Today, there is a substantial amount of time and effort devoted to risk assessment from one perspective or another, ranging from the statistical odds of actual loss to the chances of running afoul of governance rules and regulations. I am not an expert in the science of risk assessment. In my experience, the main prerequisite for exploring the possibility of the need to take a new or greater risk was the unsettled feeling that things ought to be better, that the future was indeed in some jeopardy unless we took some action—even worse, that we were missing an opportunity. I would get very uncomfortable from time to time at The Coca-Cola Company whenever things seemed to be going awfully well. Like the Russians say, "Having things too good is also not good."

I must have irritated quite a few people when, with considerable regularity, I'd go around asking our top people, "Tell me again why everything is so good. Isn't there something more we ought to be worrying about today in order to make sure we have something else to worry about tomorrow?"

> *"The world belongs to the discontented."*
> —Oscar Wilde

ROBERT WOODRUFF, the patriarch and real builder of the modern Coca-Cola Company, was fond of the Oscar Wilde admonition "The world belongs to the discontented." He quoted it often.

Coca-Cola was founded in 1886. In 1930, even with years of success behind it, Woodruff was discontented. He wanted to consolidate the then-fledgling foreign business and expand even further in the international market. Understandably, the board of directors thought it was not at all the right time for such adventuring. The stock market had just crashed in 1929. Germany and Italy and Japan were all rattling their sabers. Extreme uncertainty was the only certainty.

So what did Woodruff do? He did what today would raise eyebrows. But in those pre-SEC days Woodruff took an enormous personal risk. He circumvented the board, went to New York, and established the separate Coca-Cola Export Corporation. I can't imagine where Coke would be today if he hadn't done that. Certainly it would not be doing business in more than two hundred countries around the globe.

The Export Corporation was pretty much independent until about 1973. During those forty-three years the company's top domestic executives hardly ever interacted with international executives. Woodruff gave individuals he selected a ticket to a foreign outpost and some money and didn't see them again until they determined when and how a Coca-Cola business could be built. Communications around the globe were slow and erratic. The business had to be built on trust. That set a strong precedent and created an enduring international management philosophy for years to come.

I remember being in Japan in 1964 with the man Woodruff had selected to found our business in that country. He would get all these memos and directives from the headquarters staff, glance at them, and most of them ended up in the wastebasket. He knew that he had the trust and support of management at the highest levels and that was all that mattered.

One other risk that Woodruff took during the 1930s was perhaps even more important than the move to expand in the export market.

As the Great Depression wore on to the depths of 1933, businesses were failing, the stock market remained down, a quarter of all able-bodied American men were flat out of work. Most experts agreed that prospects for renewed prosperity in this country were very dim. Yet against this bleak landscape, Woodruff raised the advertising budget for the company to $4.3 million, a staggering record sum for the time.

We should all be pleased that he did because it was during the 1930s that the rosy-cheeked, chubby Santa Claus we all know and love was created by the artist Haddon Sundblom for a series of ads that ran every Christmas. Prior to these ads, Santa was a rather austere figure who looked like he would just as soon bring you a lump of coal for Christmas if you'd been the least bit naughty. Thanks to Woodruff's multimillion-dollar risk taking we all got a much kinder, gentler, cuddly Santa—and Coca-Cola sales soared.

Over time, many, many successful companies have failed to take important risks at critical points, and they have paid a price. Some have merely stumbled and found later redemption, but quite a few have not only fallen but disappeared. In the 1980s alone, 230 companies disappeared from the *Fortune* 500. In fact, only 16 of the 100 largest companies that were around in the early 1900s are still with us. Who knows how many of the tombstones in the graveyard of capitalism should bear the epitaph "Here lies a company that died risk free."

Perhaps one of the most dramatic and widely studied business histories of risks taken, and subsequently risks not taken, is the well-known story of Xerox. It has a full measure of both triumph and tragedy.

Xerox's roots go all the way back to 1906, when it was known as the Haloid Company. As such, they had been successfully manufacturing photographic paper in Rochester, New York, for forty-one years when, in 1947, they took a big risk on a revolutionary idea that everyone else had passed up. Chester Carlson, a relatively obscure inventor from Queens, New York, had spent years trying to interest anyone in his "electrophotographic" copying. "Carbon paper works just fine," people said, and more than twenty companies, including IBM and General Electric, turned down Carlson. They greeted his invention with what he described as "an enthusiastic lack of interest."

Carlson eventually contracted with the Battelle

Memorial Institute in Columbus, Ohio, to help refine his process. There Haloid found the invention and obtained a license to develop and market a copying machine based on Carlson's technology. A professor of classical languages at Ohio State University is credited with the term "xerography," derived from the Greek words for "dry" and "writing."

When I first came to know Haloid-Xerox, as they had been renamed, they were a moderately sized, rather stodgy firm. There was nothing pretentious about them. Their offices in Rochester had plain rubber-tile floors and metal desks and they were populated with engineers wearing plastic pocket protectors and earnest expressions. But there was an atmosphere of excitement about the place and a mood of passionate dedication.

Then in 1958, a decade after taking on Carlson's idea, a plain beige and brown metal box rolled off the pilot assembly line. It was the world's first automatic plain-paper copier, and when it was launched in 1959 as the Xerox 914, suddenly, in offices across the nation carbon paper became a quaint relic of bygone days. And a new noun, a "Xerox," and to the chagrin of their trademark attorneys a verb, "to Xerox," entered the global lexicon.

The 914 went on to become one of the world's most successful industrial products. More than two hundred thousand units were made between 1959 and 1976, the year the company stopped production of the 914. Today, the Xerox 914 is part of American history as an artifact in the Smithsonian Institution.

Xerox had grown to more than $1 billion in revenue in less than ten years based on taking a risk on a single technology. Then they temporarily lost their way because they stopped taking risks—on their own inventions, no less.

They moved their headquarters out of Rochester to the more glamorous Stamford, Connecticut. The rubber-tile floors gave way to thick carpets and the metal desks were replaced with fine wood ones. Most of the people at headquarters were "box" guys. They had grown up and grown rich with the boxy Xerox copiers, and selling more copiers was how they saw the future unfolding.

Meanwhile, in 1970, the company had set up a research facility in Palo Alto, California. In 1973 the facility demonstrated the Alto. It was the first "personal computer," with a graphics-oriented monitor with icons, overlapping "pages" on the screen, and a funny little thing called a mouse.

At that moment Xerox had at least a five-year head start over its future rivals. But the box guys at headquarters failed to take a risk. That, as I said, is one of the major diseases of success. Two others are complacency and arrogance. Engineers who finally left the Palo Alto Research Center to sign on with firms such as Apple and

Microsoft complained that they couldn't even get the attention of the top managers in the thickly carpeted offices in Stamford.

By the late 1990s, Xerox had lost its leadership in copiers and was posting losses and announcing large layoffs. In 2002 the SEC charged the firm with accounting irregularities and several of its executives with securities fraud. As of this writing, however, Xerox is still with us, reinventing itself under new management.

Here we have a proud company, built on technological innovation, so swept up in its success with one kind of product that it completely failed to take a risk on new opportunities springing up within its own ranks, albeit on the other side of the continent. They ignored the simple truth that to create profits in the long term requires innovation in the short term.

Of course, the way forward will always generate some failures. Walter Isaacson in his wonderful biography of Einstein tells a story about what Einstein said he needed in his new office at Princeton: a desk or a table, a chair, some pencils, paper, and a very large wastebasket "for all the mistakes I will make." In business, you can make a good argument for mistakes like Steve Jobs's Lisa or Power MacCube because the highly creative Apple environment that spawned them also produced big winners like iPod and iPhone. You can even justify those mistakes that have become the folkloric case studies in how-not-to-do-it courses in business schools all over the country, such as the Edsel or 45 rpm records or even New Coke. These failures, for all the valuable lessons that they teach us in hindsight about management blunders, are simply risks that just didn't work out. Such miscalculations, costly though they might be at the time, are part of the price of staying in business. As Peter Drucker pointed out nearly fifty years ago, it is management's major task to prudently risk a company's present assets in order to ensure its future existence. In fact, if a company never has a failure, I submit that their management is probably not discontented enough to justify their salaries.

Xerox was not discontented in any way. They were very, very comfortable, and, as I've noted, when you're comfortable, the temptation to quit taking risks is so great, it's almost irresistible. And failure is almost inevitable.

## Commandment Two

# Be Inflexible

> *"I'm in favor of leaving the status quo the way it is."*
> —Yogi Berra

NOT TAKING A RISK and being inflexible are closely related, but there is an important nuance of difference. The truly inflexible people are not avoiding risks. They are not merely reluctant to take a risk on some change or innovation. They are so set in their ways, so sure that they have *the* formula for success that they simply cannot see any other way of doing things. That happened at The Coca-Cola Company.

In a 1920 dispute over the use of the Coca-Cola name, a case that went all the way up to the U.S. Supreme Court, Justice Oliver Wendell Holmes ruled in favor of Coca-Cola, describing it as "a single thing from a single source and well-known to the community."

The company became so enamored of this description that it became almost biblical writ, so dogmatically accepted and jealously guarded that the source of the product began to be just as much a part of its exclusivity as the thing itself. Management was incapable of envisioning Coca-Cola as anything but "Coca-Cola"—and here's the key to our myopia—"Coca-Cola *in the familiar green bottle.*" Company leaders came to view the drink and the bottle as one and the same. There was, of course, the iconic bell-shaped fountain glass, but it was never trademarked like the contour bottle.

In all the advertising for nearly half a century the beverage and the bottle were shown together. From Santa Claus to Eisenhower, everybody was clutching that beautiful green container. We would not, could not, did not change our package—that six-and-a-half-ounce iconic green bottle. That six-and-a-half-ounce green, curvaceous bottle was how God meant Coca-Cola to be sold—"a single thing"—and by God that's how we would sell it no matter what consumers wanted! By the end of World War II at Coca-Cola, executives were so firmly set in their ways they could have stopped the growth of the business.

Coca-Cola wasn't born in the bottle. It was concocted in 1886 by one John S. Pemberton at Jacobs' Pharmacy, an Atlanta drugstore. For years its origin dictated the way Coca-Cola was sold—in a glass, only over drugstore soda fountains. The Coca-Cola syrup, the sweet caramel-colored base of the drink, was mixed with cold carbonated water and consumed on the spot. Today Coke is still sold the same way as a fountain drink in paper or plastic cups at sporting events, in theaters, through quick service food outlets such as McDonald's and many thousands of outlets all over the world, but far more gallons of Coke are now sold in supermarkets and other retail outlets in bottles and cans.

Pemberton died in 1888 and the young Coca-Cola Company passed into the hands of Asa Candler, who continued to expand the business across the southern United States, but only through pharmacies. In the late nineteenth century, the soft-drink bottling process was rather primitive and sometimes dangerous with frequent explosions. Understandably, the early founders of the business in Atlanta didn't see much future in branching out beyond soda fountain sales. (Why take the risk? See Commandment One.)

But in 1899, Benjamin Thomas and Joseph White-head, a couple of adventurous young lawyers from Chattanooga, came to Candler proposing to bottle the drink, offering to assume any of the risks. Because they saw no future in bottles, Candler agreed and literally gave away the bottling rights. Thomas and Whitehead bought the franchise to bottle Coca-Cola in perpetuity for the princely sum of just one dollar. Candler would, of course, retain the formula for the syrup and if anything came of the harebrained scheme, he'd still make money selling the syrup to the bottler or bottlers.

The bottle caught on. By 1905 there were more than two hundred bottling plants in the United States and Coca-Cola was being sold in bottles in all kinds of places, especially in the hot summer months when the small grocery stores and general stores of the time would set out large galvanized washtubs filled with ice and cold water and stocked with many different soft drinks, of which Coca-Cola was just one. There were root beers and ginger ales and orange drinks and cream sodas all together, all bottled in the same generic, eight-ounce bottle. If you reached into the tub you couldn't tell what drink you were getting, and if the label had come off in the water, the mystery was further compounded.

Prodded by bottlers, The Coca-Cola Company, which was beginning to recognize the potential of selling Coke in bottles, commissioned the Root Glass Company to design a distinctive bottle that would incorporate the Coca-Cola trademark. They wanted a bottle that you could "feel"—something you could immediately identify by touch in those tubs of cold water.

Root came up with a unique bottle made of green glass in a unique shape, a reverse hourglass figure with a fat middle and indented sides. It was a big success with the bottlers and the customers. And it became indistinguishable, in the minds of many, from the product itself.

And, as I said, that was the trouble.

As Robert Woodruff carried out his aggressive global expansion of The Coca-Cola Company, the six-and-a-half-ounce green bottle was so entrenched that he and many others did not see any other packaging possibilities. In their view, the bottle and the Coca-Cola in it were like an egg. The shell and the contents were one, inseparable, a single thing bearing the singular trademark, Coca-Cola.

Meanwhile, in 1939, at Pepsi-Cola a marketing genius named Walter Mack came up with a brilliant slogan: "Twice as much for a nickel, too." They began to sell Pepsi-Cola in twelve-ounce bottles. The slogan was everywhere, including all over the radio via one of the catchiest jingles ever written.

> *"Pepsi Cola hits the spot.*
> *Twelve full ounces, that's a lot.*
> *Twice as much for a nickel, too.*
> *Pepsi Cola is the drink for you."*
> Pepsi Jingle

PEPSI SALES began to rise.

But The Coca-Cola Company wouldn't budge. In fact, in communications within The Coca-Cola Company, Pepsi-Cola was not even referred to by its name. It was called "the imitator."

Twice as much for a nickel from the imitator was growing in popularity among more and more U.S. consumers who were able to buy refrigerators after the war and were serving more and more drinks at home. Pepsi sales doubled from 1947 to 1954 while Coca-Cola sales idled along. To be sure, Coca-Cola still outsold the competitor by a significant margin, but the gap was narrowing and a major competitor got a leg up.

But the leadership of The Coca-Cola Company was adamant. They would not consider any other packages. Besides, they reasoned, with twice as much product and twice as much expensive sugar in every bottle, Pepsi would soon go broke.

It didn't.

Finally, in 1955, faced with sharply declining supermarket sales, the inflexibility of The Coca-Cola Company gave way. The company introduced three new packages: the King-Sized ten-ounce, the twelve-ounce, and the twenty-six-ounce Family Size.

Many of our bottlers were also inflexible.

In 1974, when I was president of our U.S.A. operation, it became absolutely critical for everyone's survival that the bottlers let us change their contractual arrangements with the company. It was in their best interests but some just didn't see it that way. They were fixed in the past and would not budge.

Our bottler system was successful but antiquated. The original bottling territories were carved out in the late nineteenth and early twentieth centuries and were based on how far one could go out and get back in a single day with a horse and wagon. The preservation of territorial integrity was valid, but large chain store customers had operations that spanned across many bottlers' territories and it was becoming more and more difficult to maintain a common price. By the end of the 1960s the company's ability to serve large grocery chains was severely limited. Yet many bottlers didn't want to sell, move, or merge. And they held contracts that were granted in perpetuity. By being inflexible without realizing it, the Coca-Cola bottlers were slowly weakening the system that was, in fact, their lifeblood.

For The Coca-Cola Company to stay in business in the United States we had to raise prices and our contracts with bottlers prohibited it. In addition we had to have bottler territories that were compatible with the needs of our chain store customers. The Coca-Cola Company had to renegotiate with all of our bottlers. Under then company president Luke Smith, we began the process.

Luke Smith and I talked with every bottler owner. The bottlers often didn't take kindly to change. Folklore around the company had it that the last thing a dying bottler would say to his son or daughter was "Don't let them fool around with the contract." And we were fooling around with the contract.

Eventually, one by one, most bottler leaders recognized that if we didn't change things we were all committing corporate suicide. The world's best-known product, Coca-Cola, was in danger and we all had to work together to save it. And we did.

When the conditions around you change, remain inflexible. Keep on keeping on. Stand firm. You will fail.

> *"For this is the tragedy of man—circumstances change, but he doesn't."*
> —Machiavelli

THERE ARE SO MANY examples of severe pigheaded inflexibility in companies that once represented a leading edge of innovation that they are simply too numerous to count. We've all seen people in high places in high-tech firms sitting back in a self-satisfied, thumb-sucking mode, assuring one another that everything was wonderful while the business itself was beginning a dance toward slow death.

I was on an advisory board of IBM World Trade Americas during the 1970s and on into the mid-1980s and everything was wonderful at IBM. In sales, profits, patents—by every measure, they defined their industry. They were the best of the *Fortune* 500. Executives took sabbaticals. The mainframe computer was the future, as it always had been and always would be. And for a very long while they were right. In 1980 they projected that by 1995 revenues would exceed $250 billion. In fact, in

1984, IBM had the greatest after-tax profit of any company, any time in history, nearly $6.6 billion. Nine years later, in January 1993, IBM announced the greatest corporate loss up to that time, around $8 billion.

What happened was that IBM was completely set in its ways. They knew what was going on in the world of computers and by 1981 had developed a successful PC. But they didn't really believe in it. They believed in an internal forecast of worldwide PC sales at less than 250,000 units by 1987. In fact, more than a million were sold by 1985. Leaders at IBM didn't understand, or refused to understand, that marketing PCs was completely different from the selling and servicing of the big mainframe battleships that had given IBM global dominance. Like the military admirals and generals who are always preparing to fight the last war, the IBM management remained, in their hearts, absolutely committed to a mainframe way of thinking.

Through the 1980s, I would from time to time mention that I was seeing more and more PCs in various offices of The Coca-Cola Company, and invariably I was met with a polite smile and a shrug. It was like IBM management was standing on the bank of a river. No matter how long you stand there, you never see the same river twice—it is in constant motion. History is downstream—the future is upstream, where opportunity and danger may be on their way. But the reality was that the executives at IBM were too busy looking downstream, happily watching those beautiful, profitable mainframes floating down the river and around the world.

The final curtain on this little business history episode is that the ThinkPad, IBM's PC, ended up in the laptop factories of China under the brand name Lenovo. It's sad because IBM had such a head start. They've recovered, of course, but it wasn't easy.

Throughout the relatively new and growing computer industry there were quite a number of firms that though they had been founded in a burst of innovative creativity were nevertheless surprisingly quick to adopt an inflexible stance, and they were not nearly so fortunate as IBM. They did not survive at all.

One legendary name that many readers will remember is—was—Digital Equipment Corporation. Founded in 1958 by a couple of brilliant engineers out of MIT, Ken Olsen and Harlan Anderson, at its peak in the 1980s, DEC was the second-largest computer company in the world with about one hundred thousand employees and a highly vaunted reputation for technological genius. They were one of the first businesses connected to the Internet and they created AltaVista, one of the first comprehensive search engines. They had internal e-mail long before its market value was recognized. Work on an MP3-type personal music player began in their research center. In short, they were ahead of their time in many areas. What brought them down was the conviction that they had the *one right approach*. Everything they did was "DEC-centric," very proprietary. For all their brilliance, the DEC founders simply refused to adapt to the new, broader-based structure of the computer business. Piece by piece the company was sold off, the last of it in 1998, though I understand the logo survived for a short while in an IT company in India.

Inflexibility is a very crippling disease.

Probably there is no better example of the affliction in full fever than in the behavior of a brilliant man who literally changed the American culture—Henry Ford.

Ford did not become the nation's richest man by inventing the automobile or mass production, although he spent his life producing the first by an ever-improving use of the latter. What made Henry Ford a genius was his instinctive sense of mass marketing. He saw better than anyone at the time that if he could drive the cost down, the automobile could be transformed from a plaything of the rich into transportation for the masses. In order to do so he took two risks. First, he kept reducing the profit per car in order to increase sales volume. Second, when the average wage for an automobile assembly-line worker was less than $2.50 a day, he announced in 1914 that he would pay his workers the unheard-of wage of $5.00 a day.

Current business jargon includes the term "prosumer," those customers who both produce and consume products and services. Ford anticipated this concept by nearly a century. In paying five dollars a day, overnight Ford increased the size of his market by paying his workers enough money to actually buy the product they were making, and, more important, he bought the loyalty of a workforce that was notoriously unstable. The conventional wisdom throughout the auto industry at the time was that high turnover was unavoidable. Ford proved the conventional wisdom wrong.

Yet in a very few years, this genius who had been a visionary became so inflexible that he nearly ruined the company.

He reportedly said, regarding the Model T, "They can have it in any color they want, as long as it's black." For a long time that was just fine. But then people began to get tired of the black tin lizzies. Yet even as America was roaring into the 1920s with bigger, faster, fancier, brightly painted automobiles, Henry Ford kept insisting that the Model T, essentially unchanged since 1908, was still what America wanted and needed and he was not going to change his mind.

Inevitably, upstarts like Chevrolet and Dodge began to erode Ford's market and seriously challenge the company's dominant leadership. At last, more rational minds prevailed and Ford admitted the need to produce a better vehicle. After shutting down his main plant for six months, he successfully launched the Model A in 1928. But Henry Ford's inflexibility had brought the company to the brink of disaster and cost it a competitive edge that it has never regained.

In more recent years, during the 1980s and 1990s, both GM and Ford continued to rely on their large, gas-eating sport utility vehicles while the emerging market dominator, Toyota, began to develop their successful, high-mileage hybrid cars. Jim Press, the former president of Toyota North America, said, "Both of us had the same tea leaves, the same research—is fuel going to become more plentiful or less plentiful? Is the air going to become cleaner or more polluted? Do you do something proactive and innovative to be in tune with where society is going? Or do you hold on to where it has been and then don't let go, to the bitter end?"*

The story of each company, each industry that failed is different, of course. Some are more straightforward than others. It's obvious, when you look back, that in the early part of the twentieth century, no matter how they resisted, ice companies would have to find something else to do because they were going to be replaced by electrical refrigeration. It's not quite so obvious how the majority of more than three thousand bicycle companies just disappeared while others morphed into the

---

*Quoted in "Murder, Starvation, & Catastrophe," an address by Richard Demillo, dean of the college of computing, Georgia Tech, Februrary 28, 2007.

automobile business and even, as the Wright Brothers demonstrated, into the airframe business. Clearly some folks were more flexible than others.

However, there really is no question as to what caused the demise of what was once the outstanding pioneer in its field. Montgomery Ward invented catalog sales. The company died because of the inflexibility of one man.

Montgomery Ward was run into the ground by one inflexible, flinty lawyer, Sewell Avery. Avery had saved the firm during the Great Depression by severely cutting back when others were expanding. The trouble was, Avery carried the Depression mentality with him the rest of his life. "Gloomy Sewell," they called him. His calendar was firmly set on the year 1929. A crash was always just a few days away.

After World War II when new households were being formed in new developments like Levittown, Avery not only failed to see the emerging prosperity. He *refused* to see it. By the mid-1950s, teenagers' weekly allowances began to exceed the American family's entire disposable income in 1940. The country was rich and getting richer. But Avery was so inflexible that he simply would not acknowledge the post–World War II economic boom that was all around him. He would not invest in or expand the business in any way. As a result, in the ten years following the war, while Ward's rival, Sears, was doubling its sales, Ward's sales declined 10 percent.

Montgomery Ward as such no longer exists. Meanwhile, the inflexible Mr. Avery went to his grave insisting that severe depression was just around the corner. He believed what he believed and could not be convinced otherwise. In fact, he was notoriously brutal in firing those who kept trying to lift the curtain on reality for him.

Another example of just plain dumb inflexibility is Republic Steel. In the 1960s, one of the major customers of Republic Steel was the canning industry, which was beginning to turn to lighter-weight, cheaper-to-ship aluminum. Republic was very rich and successful. It would have been logical for them to get into the aluminum business themselves, and they could have easily done so at the time by tapping into their large cash reserves and purchasing an existing aluminum company. Instead, the company leaders at Republic were so inflexible they announced that they would never give up on steel cans. They even referred to aluminum as "the weak metal," and they fought its encroachment into their canning market with everything they had. Eventually, everything they had was gone. Republic Steel is no more.

Or for sheer unenlightened stubbornness just consider Hollywood's attitude toward television in those early days when I was bumbling along with a primitive talk show at WOW-TV in Omaha. How did big, rich Hollywood greet the new baby? They were utterly contemptuous. The joke was: "Vaudeville died and television was the little box they put it in."

The major studios wanted nothing to do with the silly business. Let has-been burlesque comics like Milton Berle have the toy. The big screen and motion pictures was the future and always would be, according to them. Mainstream Hollywood made fun of television and television people and they were delighted when Newton Minow described TV as a "vast wasteland." They even boycotted the medium in the hope that it would somehow just disappear. Apparently, no one liked television except the American people.

Eventually, of course, the studios had to embrace it, but their initial inflexible stance created unnecessary conflicts between "movie people" and "TV people," sometimes within the same companies—not to mention enormous lost opportunities. Instead of becoming the driving force that they could have been in developing television, the major studios became, at their worst, obstructionist stumbling blocks or, at best, bystanders.

One of the most perverse examples of inflexibility is the entire airline industry.

In the 1930s and 1940s, no technical marvel more eloquently symbolized the age of modern transportation than the shining airliners whisking important people from coast to coast in a matter of hours. Not only was this an exciting and innovative way to travel, but soon it was also being innovatively marketed. Pan Am's Juan Trippe introduced "tourist class" tickets. No longer was air travel exclusively reserved for glamorous movie stars and Wall Street tycoons. The age of mass travel on wings was under way.

But after their bold beginning, for years the industry languished. The planes got bigger and faster but the pace of innovation in the business itself slowed to a crawl. Protected for decades from the vicissitudes of the free market by strict government regulations, they forgot how to be entrepreneurial businesspeople. They became rigidly inflexible in how they did business even when confronted with ever-mounting losses. They kept doing the same things over and over again, with the same dismal results, sliding in and out of bankruptcy, making the same promises of better management and improved efficiency. In truth, some within the industry have blamed the whole situation on the ease with which airlines were able to operate while bankrupt. It is indeed a complicated business with an interlocking mixture of public and private interests. Nevertheless, from my viewpoint the only strategy airline management seemed to be trying was to continue to seek cost-cutting wage concessions from their workers. (In my experience, in the absence of other strategic changes, the truism is true—you can never cost cut your way to profitability.)

Then along came an innovative, flamboyant entrepreneur named Herb Kelleher. He founded a new airline that resembled the established airlines in only one respect—he transported people on airplanes. He changed almost everything else. To begin with, his whole fleet was just one kind of airplane, the 737, so service on the aircraft was simplified and streamlined. He changed the way routes were laid out and the way seats were assigned. He changed pricing and even went after different customers. The result? Southwest Airlines made profits in an industry that some investors had already pronounced hopeless. (It remains to be seen as this is being written whether Southwest can remain profitable in the face of today's ever-rising fuel costs and the resulting cost-cutting measures.)

To fail, then, be inflexible. However, I want to be clear about this: Flexibility is not a virtue in and of itself. Neither is it a shield for the fainthearted to hide behind in order to waffle around and never make a hard decision. Flexibility and the ability to adapt is an essential attribute of leadership that goes beyond simple managerial, operational skills, or technical competence. I believe that flexibility is a continual, deeply thoughtful process of examining situations and, when warranted, quickly adapting to changing circumstances. It is, in essence, the key to Darwin's whole notion of the survival of the fittest. Flexibility. Adaptation.

> *"The man who never alters his opinion is like standing water, and it breeds reptiles of the mind."*
> —William Blake

I'll ADMIT, some organizations have been able to resist change for generations. I remember talking with Bing Crosby when he was working with us. He was certainly one of the most widely loved and successful entertainers of his time. He also owned shares of the Minute Maid Company. After The Coca-Cola Company acquired Minute Maid, we persuaded Bing to do some commercials in the late 1960s. Bing was an avid golfer, and asked us, because of Robert Woodruff's long association with Augusta National Golf Club, if he could become a member.

The response given to Mr. Woodruff by the czar of Augusta National was: "We don't take show folk!"

But businesses cannot afford such idiosyncratic resistance to change, and, indeed, even the most recalcitrant business leaders would certainly never actually characterize themselves as inflexible. More than likely they would pay lip service to a philosophy of change, expressing the usual platitudes about how they embrace change and welcome it. But in fact it is easy to get stuck in the comfortable rut of the status quo. Why? Well, change of any kind is difficult. Think of your own lives. Making a move to a new town can be absolutely wrenching.

But an even greater contributing *cause* of inflexibility in business is embodied in my next commandment—and is also a *symptom* of it.

# Commandment Three

## Isolate Yourself

THIS IS SO APPEALING. And it's so easy. There are just a few things you need to do to create your own executive bubble. Start with your surroundings. Build your own bubble. There's nothing like a physically isolated fortress to keep the riffraff away, so get yourself a great big office in some remote corner of the most remote executive floor and then shut the door.

I've been told of one rather colorful CEO who practically built his own Taj Mahal at corporate headquarters. Other executives shared the floor, but one entire side was carved out for him and he barricaded himself deep within. His suite was protected by its own set of heavy plate-glass doors, which opened into a waiting room guarded by a receptionist on an elevated dais in front of another set of wooden doors. Behind those doors was the CEO's actual office, an exotic, decidedly weird space, with dramatic Brazilian artwork, New Age background music, and the aroma of burning scented candles. A wall of TV monitors completed the scene. Imagine what a stressful impact this CEO's altar to his ego might have had on a middle-level field executive coming into headquarters to discuss a bit of bad news! One look and there is just no way he'd have the nerve to say a word.

Once protected, never leave your bubble except to visit other people who have their own bubbles. For heaven's sake, don't answer your own phone. Ever. Don't even find out where the copy machine is located. Above all, don't walk around the headquarters offices and talk to people. I would wander around on various floors and just drop in on people, introduce myself, ask how they were doing, what they were doing, what we might be doing better.

Of course, if you want to be isolated, don't do this. It's a complete waste of time. People invariably burden you with some detail of the daily business that you're better off not knowing. Like their names. Don't bother learning the names of employees. They might leave, and then you've wasted all that effort. (I read once of an eccentric upper-class British matron who never bothered to learn the servants' names. Down through several changes of butlers, she simply called each new one "Butler." The maid, "Maid." Gardener, "Gardener." She would have made an excellent, isolated CEO.)

Unfortunately for those who wish to remain isolated, the history of most successful businesses runs counter to this disposition. In fact, one of the traits of many of the legendary builders of business was that they had an uncanny ability to know and relate to their employees at every level. Dwayne Wallace, who built the Cessna Aircraft Company through the 1960s and 1970s, was reputed to be able to walk the assembly line of the Wichita plant and not only know every one of about three thousand employees by name but also know something about their families. This hands-on, personal touch is no doubt impossible in a global operation today, but it is certainly a worthy and attainable goal within a fairly large headquarters staff. But if you want to be isolated, forget it.

If you want to be even more thoroughly isolated, hire a good personal caterer and follow my strict isolationist diet.

Always eat lunch with a few close members of your immediate staff in the executive dining room. One particularly arrogant CEO followed my strict isolationist diet religiously. Every single day he ate a catered lunch on the top floor of his headquarters building with just his top executives. The dissatisfaction boiling up on the floors below and among the stockholders was not allowed to interfere with his digestive process. To his credit, this executive did succeed in increasing revenues, but his management style did more long-term harm than good, alienating employees, customers, and stockholders. Even if the top executives who lunched with him daily were the only true believers in what he was trying to accomplish, simple common sense tells you that these happy few would not, ultimately, be enough to get the job done.

An imperious style is usually counterproductive. How the leaders of a business relate to the workforce does matter. Being isolated alienates, breeds rumors, and, after a time, even revolt. But if you want to fail, it's a winning strategy.

For further isolation—surround yourself with a collection of advisers and staff who are paid to think you are wonderful! That's their only job!

Getting the truth about anything can be difficult because you have to wend your way through layers of managers, each of whom might be tempted to bring you his own version of the truth. Therefore, avoid the process entirely. Don't step out into the marketplace. Don't even go out into the hall. Get all your information, preferably in summary form, from your trusted staff. They are there to tell you what you need to hear and to filter out what you don't need to bother about. And even if you look in the mirror and know that you're not totally wonderful, or if you have a spouse who has the annoying habit of reminding you that you are mortal, do you want to hear that from people at work? Certainly not. Keep them at a distance.

Cowed directors will also help enhance your isolation and probably your pay package. Even with stricter regulations regarding independent directors, whatever they are, it's not too hard to remind them of why they should be grateful to you. With cowed directors and solid isolation from the stockholders, you should really have no trouble with your pay, but a word of caution. Shareholders and various government entities are taking a harder look at top executives' tying pay to performance. Goodness! What a mistake! Even if you fail miserably, you should not be punished for your mistakes. In fact, your first order of business, before you ever do any work, is to make sure that you are compensated royally no matter what happens to the business. Keep any and all potential critics out of your way.

> *"It's a rare person who wants to hear what he doesn't want to hear."*
> —Dick Cavett
>
> *"Think not those faithful who praise thy words and actions but those who kindly reprove thy faults."*
> —Socrates

PUT OUT A SIGN: DON'T MAKE THE BOSS MAD. BRING ME NO BAD NEWS.

Adolf Hitler did this rather well. His secretary, Martin Bormann, quickly learned to bring the führer only pleasant tidings. Indeed, in any organization you can usually find some "good news" and someone who will happily bring it to you if it ushers him or her into the

inner luncheon circle. On the other hand, I've person-
ally found that it pays to be paranoid, getting bad news
to the top quickly so that you can quickly take steps to
avert disaster.

Charles Kettering, the great engineering genius who
helped steer General Motors during its glory years, said,
"Don't bring me anything but trouble. Good news
weakens me." I don't know that I'd go quite that far, but
the simple truth is that all progress in an organization
has to, by definition, stem from the effort to solve a
problem, which means, of course, that you have to know
about the problem before you can get to the bottom
of it.

You have to work at it.

When I would visit parts of the Coca-Cola world,
the local managers would often meet me at the airport
and take me to the three local customers where Coke
was a huge success. But I wanted to see stores that were
not on the list and would sometimes just stop the car
and jump out to go into an outlet. I also wanted to sit
down and have direct conversations with employees. I'd
say, "Here's what's on my mind. What's on your mind?"
I think I usually got pretty straight answers because I'd
often hear the same concerns from a number of people.

It's instructive that during World War II, Winston
Churchill created a special office whose sole duty was to
bring him bad news. He wanted the unvarnished truth,
no matter what it was. Hitler, on the other hand, thought

he was still winning the war until quite late in the conflict. If you want to be an effective leader, you have to find ways to break out of the isolation and bunker mentality that many bosses find so tempting.

> *"A desk is a dangerous place from which to view the world."*
> —John le Carré

CREATE A CLIMATE OF FEAR. It's so easy. It's built into every high office with the power to hire and fire, and it can happen without your even knowing it. I remember when I was in my first job that involved managing a number of salesmen for Butternut Coffee. Periodically they were supposed to come in and report to me and discuss the situation in their region. There was one salesman who was very, very good. One of the best, yet he never came into Omaha to see me. There was always some excuse: He was sick, there was an emergency with some customer, his car had thrown a rod—something.

Only by accident did I learn that even though he was performing very well, he was afraid of me. He was intimidated by just the process of coming into the headquarters and taking the elevator up to my office. I changed this dynamic by going to him, picking him up, and bringing him back with me to Omaha. He had to get to know that there was nothing to be afraid of, from me, or from the headquarters building. This individual went on to a highly successful career.

There is a great deal of difference between an environment of creative tension in an organization and a climate of fear. Creating a good working environment is hard work. It requires sensitivity to the mood and spirit of an organization, but it pays off. It's no accident that many firms consistently listed on *Fortune*'s list of the 100 Best Companies to Work for in America are also consistently among those delivering the best shareholder return.

An environment of fear, on the other hand, requires so little effort I really think it must be quite tempting. You don't have to understand anything to inculcate it. Just scream, throw tantrums. Dress down people who make mistakes in front of other people. Embarrass them. Be rude. Act like a two-year-old. Sadly, there are plenty of managers who do. They're even proud of the outrageous demands they make on their underlings— proud of treating the help badly. In my opinion not one of them is "creative" enough to justify it, even if they are editors of fashion magazines or directors of motion pictures or one of the hottest new turnaround artists in industry. Bad behavior is bad behavior and inexcusable. We all can remember times when we lost our cool, where we have been unfair, but in each instance we diminished ourselves. I can't deny that sometimes you'll get short-term success and even publicity.

In the early 1990s, the media heaped loads of praise on the newest tough turnaround hero, Al Dunlap, aka "Chainsaw Al," the self-styled "Rambo in Pinstripes." He fired a flock of people and pared every expense to the bone. *BusinessWeek* pointed out that Al had anointed himself as America's best CEO. Quite a few business reporters seemed to buy the hype. That was just before he drove a fine company called Sunbeam into the ground in 1998.

To completely isolate yourself, put yourself first in all things. When there is credit to be taken, take *all* of it. When there is blame to be taken, take *none* of it. If the spotlight of public attention turns toward your company in a friendly way, leap into that light and leave your employees and associates and everyone else who might have given you a helping hand way off in the wings somewhere. After you have taken all the credit for some corporate accomplishment, in the unlikely event that you harbor some feelings of guilt, you can easily assuage those by sending your hardest workers a nice Christmas poinsettia or a holiday turkey. Small engraved crystal paperweights with the worker's name and a "thank you" over your signature can also be quite touching.

Hogging the limelight is not an absolute guarantee of failure, but it does contribute to that extreme isolation that can make great success very difficult.

Among some of the most successful people I've known well and worked with I've found there is often a self-effacing quality—an avoidance of the spotlight. If you read Warren Buffett's annual letters to his shareholders you can't cover more than a couple of paragraphs before you find him lavishing praise and great credit on someone else. Likewise, Herbert A. Allen of Allen & Company is similarly eager to make others in his company the stars of any favorable publicity. It is only when things go wrong or are not as good as they might have been that both of these men take center stage to assume responsibility.

In all walks of your life, talk only to those who agree with you, preferably to other CEOs. At conferences and board meetings—in the clubs you join and the parties you attend—find like-minded, well-off birds of a feather. Look to your peers for ideas and opinions, political viewpoints, and especially rates of pay. In my own experience, I found that I consistently had to make an extra effort to broaden my acquaintances. This isn't as easy as it might sound.

If you've got some lofty title on your door, the crowd of those who will disagree with you thins out pretty rapidly. That's why I like the story about John Wooden, the legendary UCLA basketball coach. He was a man of firm convictions and he was a winner. But in his sixteenth season, while he'd made it to the NCAA tournament every year, he had yet to win a championship. In 1963, Jerry Norman, Wooden's highly opinionated assistant coach, began to question absolutely everything

Wooden had been doing. That was heresy—tantamount to fomenting revolution, yet Norman somehow persuaded Wooden to apply virtually all new tactics to his game. The upshot was that UCLA won the 1964 NCAA title and went on to win nine of the next eleven tournaments. Wooden subsequently said, "Whatever you do in life, surround yourself with smart people who'll argue with you."

That's one of the reasons I am a strong believer in management teams. When teams of leaders complement and balance one another (as in the cases of Warren Buffett and Charlie Munger at Berkshire Hathaway, Tom Murphy and Dan Burke at CapCities, or Frank Wells and Michael Eisner at Disney), then one person's shortcomings can often be offset by another's strengths. But when there is only room for one dominant personality in the room, then watch out because what he or she *is* that's what the company is; and if he or she isn't enough, then the company is doomed.

Watch out for bright lights that surround themselves with dim bulbs!

I was very fortunate at Coca-Cola in that I had several very, very bright top executives working for me who would not hesitate to tell me they thought I was not only wrong but dead wrong! I also had some strong-minded secretaries. They were so nervy they would sometimes bring letters back to me with a sweet smile and that marvelous expression my high school paper's editor used to use: "Are you sure you want to say this?" Usually I didn't. That's the wonderful thing about letters versus e-mail. You have time to think. More on that later.

Assume the whole world lives as you do. Hubert Humphrey once suggested that every member of Congress and every high public official should be required to take public transportation once a week so they would know how the world really lives. This should also apply to top business leaders. It helps to remember the old adage: "I may be the CEO at the office, but I take out the garbage at home."

Some old-timers in the company once told me about a third-generation Coca-Cola bottler from New England who came from an old aristocratic family. He'd probably never even been inside the plant—probably hadn't even tasted a Coke in years. Nevertheless, he felt qualified to question the company's wisdom in advertising on the radio on late Sunday afternoons. "No one is listening to the radio on Sunday afternoons," he said. "Everyone is out playing polo." That's pure isolation! That's the way to keep your own self foremost in mind and completely lose touch with your customers, employees, and shareholders. And best of all—you don't even know it!

If you follow Commandment Three and effectively isolate yourself, you will not only *not know what you don't know* about your business, but you will remain supremely and serenely confident that what you do know is right. Isolation, carried to its most extreme form, tends to breed a sense of almost divine right. People like Henry Ford and Sewell Avery and a host of the managers of some of the highly successful enterprises that we mentioned such as Xerox and IBM became convinced that they were not only right, but even more deadly, they began to believe, at times anyway, that they could do no wrong. When the encyclicals coming out of a corporate headquarters proclaim, "We can do no wrong, we know best!" watch out because the leaders of the business are advancing confidently into the tantalizing allure of my next commandment.

# Commandment Four

## Assume Infallibility

To BEGIN WITH, never ever admit a problem or a mistake. If something seems to be heading in the wrong direction, cover up, or, better yet, wait until you have a full-blown crisis, then blame it on some external force—or blame it on somebody else. Customers are frequently troublesome. You can always blame whatever goes wrong on them!

Annual reports often amuse me, particularly the letters to shareholders. In one report after another, even if the company has had a thoroughly disastrous year, the chairman's letter is frequently an artful exercise in finger-pointing at any number of causes ranging from unforeseen currency fluctuations to the unusually active hurricane season. You have certainly read, many times probably, that all-purpose feckless homage to passive impotence, "Mistakes were made." The timbers are caving in, dust is in the air, and the person in charge of it all blithely asserts, "Mistakes were made." Implied, of course, is, "But not by me."

That's the refreshing thing about Warren Buffett's

legendary annual letters as chairman of Berkshire Hathaway. If in a particular year, performance is not quite up to previous years or what might have been expected, Warren is quick to say, "It wasn't good and it was my fault." Despite his virtually unequaled record for profitably allocating capital, he lays no claim to infallibility. In his 1996 letter to shareholders, for example, Warren noted the problems with Berkshire's investment in USAir and commented: "In another context, a friend once asked me: 'If you're so rich, why aren't you smart?' After reviewing my sorry performance with USAir, you may conclude he had a point."

Coke again also provides an instructive example of the malady of infallibility left to fester.

In 1999, several schoolchildren in Belgium got sick and they attributed it to some Coca-Cola they'd recently consumed. The company did a bit of technical evaluation and convinced themselves at headquarters—a few thousand miles away—that there was nothing in the product that could have made the children sick. And that was that. The company was infallible in such matters.

Now, the children thought they were sick. Their parents thought they were sick. The doctors thought they were sick. Key executives in the company did not.

Sales plummeted and with agonizing slowness the company management finally forced itself to do what should have been done on the first day of the crisis—took the offending product off the shelves. Even though, as far as company leadership could tell, the Coke was completely uncontaminated. The fact is that the perception was clear and without hard facts to the contrary, perception became truth. But the pain was drawn out and the negative publicity was allowed to gather momentum. The whole affair resulted in the largest product recall in the company's 120-year history and required costly months to repair the damage to its reputation and image. Reputation and image are priceless. Guard them with your life. As it says in Proverbs: "A good name is rather to be chosen than great riches."

Schlitz beer had one of the greatest names in the American brewing business. Do you even remember it? In 1975 Schlitz was number two in the country, behind Budweiser, and it aspired to be number one. Schlitz management fancied themselves more sophisticated in the ways of marketing than the traditionalists at Anheuser-Busch. They used more extensive "marketing research" than the competition and began to see themselves as just plain smarter. They began to think that their way of doing business was infallible, and if they ran counter to the traditions of the brewing business when they cut corners to reduce their ingredients costs, well, so be it. And for a while it looked like a good idea.

And for a while things were all right.

But Schlitz kept tinkering with the brewing process. To speed up the brewing cycle, they introduced new chemicals that began to affect the quality of the beer.

When the perception of quality in even the most ordinary product is lost, all is lost. When consumers got word that Schlitz had cut corners with its ingredients, they reacted negatively. In an intensely brand-loyal business, Schlitz drinkers began to abandon their beer. From one of the leading brews in the nation, Schlitz dropped to the point in the mid-1980s where "The Beer That Made Milwaukee Famous" was not only not famous—it was gone.

The infallible we-know-best attitude of management has caused many companies to ignore reality and miss opportunities.

General Motors spent time, money, and an irretrievable part of their reputation fighting off and denying the allegations of Ralph Nader's *Unsafe at Any Speed*, a 1965 book criticizing safety throughout the automotive industry, but with one famous chapter aimed specifically at Chevrolet's new, rear-engine Corvair. Rather than meeting with Nader and other critics and addressing the possibility of working with others in the industry and perhaps improving the engineering of *all* rear-engine cars, GM executives hired private detectives who were accused of harassing Nader. The leadership of GM squandered what could have been a golden opportunity to really burnish its image of genuine concern over public safety. It chose, instead, to remain infallible at any cost—and the result was an incalculable loss of public goodwill.

Earlier I mentioned being fortunate in having a team of managers who individually would readily tell me when they thought my executive infallibility was not so infallible. One very important instance occurred right after the Berlin Wall came down in 1989.

If you want to fail, do what I did.

We were in a meeting with the head of our German operations and Claus Halle, also a German, who was head of all our international operations. During a review of a routine annual business plan, the German management team put a project on the table that called for the company to invest roughly half a billion dollars or more in this new democratic state of East Germany. The project cost cut deeply into the total budget that was being put together, and apparently I was tough, to a fault, in rejecting it. After the meeting Claus came to me and said that the head of the German management wanted to resign.

I was shocked. Why?

Claus responded, "You didn't listen clearly to what he had to say. Much of this investment would come from the German bottlers. You don't know the potential of East Germany. You've never been there. You rejected it out of hand without considering that this could be a great opportunity."

Claus went on, "At the very least, you should talk to them again. But I'd like to ask you to do more. Come with me to see East Germany for yourself, firsthand, and make up your own mind."

We went to East Germany. We went everywhere. And everywhere I saw opportunity. My mind was completely changed. We assembled everyone involved together, and I apologized for being so narrowly focused and so intransigent. Together, we made plans then and there to buy several plants in the East.

A month later at the World Economic Forum in Davos, Switzerland, I announced that the Coca-Cola system was prepared to invest a billion dollars in Eastern Europe, including East Germany. The move became a major turning point in the renewed global thrust of the company at that time and was also a breakthrough in the total investment of Western businesses in the former Soviet bloc. In addition to our capital investment in machinery for bottling and distribution operations, trucks and vending machines, Coca-Cola also acted, as it did everywhere in the world, as an economic driver, creating opportunities supporting the development of businesses related to our industry such as the manufacture of bottles, cans, crates, pallets, and printing.

Our ultimately profitable experience in East Germany and the rest of the Eastern European countries is further proof that one cannot know enough about a country or a business situation from a briefing book in the comfort of one's headquarters offices. When Neville Isdell returned to The Coca-Cola Company to become CEO in 2004, before making a single change, he spent his first hundred days just traveling all over the world, looking at operations and talking to employees and customers. I can't emphasize this simple truth enough—it really pays to see for yourself. And it pays to really listen to your own people face-to-face instead of through the filter of layers of bureaucracy.

You cannot exploit any marketing advantages you may have without knowing what's happening on the ground, what the trends are, and what matters in each location where you do business. The best source of information is from your own field force, your local team. Management policies and strategies that are simply handed down as fiat from on high are destined for failure. If you want to increase your chances of failure, deny the possibility that you are not always 100 percent perfect in your judgment. Ignore the fact that sometimes others do know a thing or two. Cast aside the wise words of Justice Oliver Wendell Holmes, "Certitude is not the test of certainty."

So, if you want to fail, pose as an infallible leader.

And if you want to fail even more spectacularly, the next commandment is just what you're looking for.

## Commandment Five

# Play the Game Close to the Foul Line

THREE YEARS AFTER I was born, the family's house burned to the ground. We lost almost everything. We had to find a new place to live and the Great Depression was bearing down. My father, Leo, forty-two years old, was literally starting over. Yet he was able to rebuild our life. We left the farm and moved to Sioux City, Iowa, where he took a job at the local stockyard, a large center where livestock were sold and traded. Gradually he worked his way up to become one of the most savvy cattle brokers in the region. He had the uncanny ability to appraise and quickly value the cattle. Ultimately, Leo would bet anyone a Stetson hat that he could look at a pen of fifty or so cattle and come within ten pounds of the average weight per head. As a teenager in the summer, I worked for him and I never saw anyone take him up on the bet. I also imagine that he never had to give away a Stetson.

But my father had something even more valuable than a savvy eye. In a business that had more than its share of con artists, he had an absolutely sterling reputation for being a straight shooter. Ranchers from western Nebraska and Wyoming and South Dakota invested their fortunes and spent months of their lives, often in terrible weather, raising a herd of cattle that they would then put on a train and call my father with the simple request, "Leo, get me the best price you can."

They trusted him implicitly. And that was a quality I wanted to emulate, to be trusted. Not feared. Not loved. But trusted—trusted to be forthright and honest with everyone—trusted to be fair—trusted to do the right thing.

If you play it close to the line you're not likely to inspire much trust on the part of your customers or employees. And you will fail.

> *"Success is more permanent when you achieve it without destroying your principles."*
> —Walter Cronkite

I MENTIONED EARLIER the role that trust played in Robert Woodruff's building of The Coca-Cola Company's global business. Trust was then, and is now, the essential foundation of any business. Despite improvements in technology and new fads in management and marketing, all business finally boils down to matters of trust—consumers trust that the product will do what it promises it is supposed to—investors trust that management is competent—employees trust management to live up to its obligations.

In recent years we seem to have quite a few smart, energetic people who have evidenced a rather fuzzy view of the right thing.

Kmart and Wal-Mart were founded in the same year, 1962. Yet Kmart pursued a dangerous path that ultimately led to bankruptcy in 2002. Along the way there were rumors and allegations of corruption and self-dealing on the part of executives. Indeed, a senior real-estate executive with the firm was convicted of bribery. The truth is they played close to the line and in some cases the courts said they crossed it.

One of the reasons corruption became more widespread, was because our whole social environment became less civil and more tolerant of bad behavior. The late senator Daniel Patrick Moynihan once described it as defining deviancy downward.

In 1969 a famous experiment was conducted by Philip Zimbardo, a Stanford psychologist. Two cars with no license plates and the hoods up were abandoned—one in the Bronx, New York, the other in Palo Alto, California. In the Bronx the car was stripped and trashed in a matter of minutes.

In Palo Alto something quite different happened. Nothing. For more than a week the car sat there unmolested. But one day the psychologist himself took a sledgehammer and began smashing the car. Soon, pass-ersby were taking turns with the hammer and within a few hours the car was demolished. This experiment led to the "broken windows" theory of crime—the idea that if a broken window is left unrepaired in a building, soon vandals will break the rest of the windows. According to the theory the broken window says, "No one cares. Break a window and nothing happens to you. Break more. It's okay."

To a degree the business environment of a few years ago was suffering a similar fate. Little cracks in the body of ethics were being ignored.

Another reason why corruption became more wide-spread is that we began to spend an inordinate amount of time catering to our valued friends who help to make "the market"—the Wall Street analysts.

For most of its 120 years in business, The Coca-Cola Company had little to do with Wall Street. The glori-ous annual reports that the company issued consisted of eight black-and-white pages on almost tissue-thin pa-per, no pictures. The company's attitude was: "What you need to know, there it is. Read it."

The leadership of the company rarely talked to the street. Public relations people were paid to keep com-pany executives' names *out* of the papers. The product was the star, not the CEO or the CFO.

Gradually, though, for The Coca-Cola Company and virtually all companies, the annual report took on a whole new meaning. It became a public relations vehicle. No longer did it just report on what the companies were doing. Now annual reports of most companies are page after page of full color, featuring people of all races, creeds, and cultures plus a double-page spread of a pristine forest in Maine that was *not* cut down to produce the report. Somewhere in all this green beauty you'll find the numbers.

In 1982 the longest bull market in history began. And with the exception of a temporary dip in 1987, it raged for eighteen years. During that time, many companies began to let the analysts into the front yard, then the hall, the kitchen, then into the living room. And finally many woke up one day and found them in the bedroom.

They were no longer there to see how companies were doing. They were there with sweet pillow talk, suggesting what the company's leadership might do.

Up until that great bull market, chief financial officers were not judged on the basis of how creative they were. They were smart, tough, and often downright mean. Their basic responsibility was to test every dollar that came in and went out to see if it was real. If they had been dealing in gold coins, they would have bitten them. Bringing good news was not their function. CFOs were the truth tellers. They didn't gild anything. You could always count on the CFO to tell the CEO the unvarnished truth, good, bad, or indifferent.

But as the stock market began to soar—and as businesses let the street into their bedrooms—slowly but surely the office of the CFO became a profit center, an important profit center. "I need another five cents this quarter. Find it!" some harassed CEOs would say.

Over time, instead of being the guardians of the transparency and the fiscal integrity of the corporation, many CFOs became the rock stars of business, and the celebrities on the street were the analysts—who, by the way, also became more and more important to the economic health of investment banking firms.

With virtually every public company talking to Wall Street all the time, there was constant demand for short-term results. Demand was so strong that pressure to achieve short-term results became almost inescapable.

A few corporate leaders found themselves no longer asking "Is it right?" but "Is it legal?" And then from that point, it was just a short leap to "Can we get away with it?"

The end of the story for these companies was tragic. People were fudging figures and cooking books to hide debt, to hype earnings, to avoid taxes—or to do all three.

For those involved the end result was disgrace and for some it was prison. For some CEOs and CFOs there was a sense of executive immunity from the moral obligations and laws that bind society. Even after Adelphia went public, John Rigas and his sons operated the company apparently as if it were the family treasure chest. High-flying companies such as Enron and Tyco were in trouble, yet they had CEOs and CFOs who acted without regard for the owners or the employees.

While the vast majority of corporations played by the rules and did not follow Commandment Five, there were quite a few others who played it so close to the line that they got chalk on their pants and occasionally stepped over the line. There were enough of these delinquent firms to span the alphabet from Adelphia to World Com. And, unfortunately, their actions generated so much bad press that they somewhat tarnished the reputation of all business. The seemingly endless photos of crooked businessmen throwing lavish parties and cavorting with the high, the mighty, and the glamorous hurt all of us.

Another part of the problem is the obsession with celebrity. It's one of the unhealthiest aspects of modern life. The camera is always on and in the world of twenty-four-hour communication, professional talkers are always looking for someone new to talk about. Some leading executives have been happy to oblige. To get their faces on the cover of a magazine they have gone to great lengths, spending fortunes on lavish entertaining and erecting gaudy homes.

When you become someone even mildly important, be careful—the writers may praise you to the heavens and endow you with more charm and more intellect than you could possibly deserve or they will find you more flawed than Scrooge. Soon after I was elected president of The Coca-Cola Company, I was the subject of some profiles in business publications. I hardly recognized myself. I was either a white knight to help lead the company or I was the living embodiment of the famous Peter Principle, promoted beyond my level of competence.

Coming from the Midwest, where even the most prosperous farmers take great pains to hide their status, it makes it somewhat easier to keep your hat size from expanding too greatly.

Everyone likes recognition, but one has to be careful not to be seduced by our cult of celebrity and tempted to cross over the line of ethical behavior.

> *"Managers are concerned with doing things right. Leaders are concerned with doing the right things."*
> —Anonymous

AFTER EVERY BURST of business scandal in this country, it seems that we create additional regulations.

The first attempt to control trading for bonds and shares followed the panic of 1792, which was triggered by unethical speculation on the part of William Duer, secretary to the board of the treasury. Alexander Hamilton, our first treasury secretary, was scrupulously honest. But his associate Duer has gone down in history with the dubious distinction of being the first American guilty of insider trading. His nefarious manipulations caused auctioneers and traders to move themselves from the coffeehouses and curbsides to a permanent central location (destined to become the New York Stock Exchange) where dealings could be better controlled and better records kept.

The scandals of Ulysses S. Grant's administration and the rigging of markets and competition by the robber barons of the late nineteenth century spawned further rules and antitrust laws. More laws were passed after Harding's Teapot Dome in the early 1920s and many more after the devastating crash of 1929. Still more regulations were enacted in subsequent decades attempting to control price fixing, bid rigging, and unfair competition.

We can never pass enough laws to make men ethical. There were already some seventy-one thousand pages of federal regulations plus SEC and New York Stock Exchange rules on the books at the time the Enron scandal broke. Laws against fraud are very clear, yet in the runup to the troubled mortgage market that came unraveled in the summer of 2007 there were Web sites where you could obtain phony identification, even get phony pay stubs, in order to secure mortgages from loan officers who should have been aware that such chicanery was not only possible but probable. The subprime crisis resulted from some very poor judgment coupled in some cases with outright criminal actions.

Today as I write this, despite stricter (some would say too strict) regulations and despite public outrage over excessive executive compensation and questionable executive behavior, we still hear about some business leaders' running close to the line.

I find this attitude difficult to understand. All I can conclude is that these leaders were and are so out of touch (see Commandment Four) that they have no sense of the common human frailties we all share—including their own.

While in the navy, toward the end of World War II, I was assigned duty in a hospital that was administering to some of the worst wounded cases: amputees, the blind, the deaf, and those who had been traumatized to the degree that they could no longer talk. My military record must have indicated something about speech experience in high school because I was put to work in the aural rehabilitation center dealing with those who had speech handicaps. I was totally unqualified, but picked up some techniques from the one other actual therapist in the hospital and together we improvised a reasonable record of patient speech recovery.

Among patients there was no rank. Enlisted men and officers were treated the same. During the rehabilitation process enlisted men battled their way back to full recovery, yet some officers who had never questioned their own abilities were reduced to broken shadows of their former selves, full of despair. My experience in this hospital made me acutely aware at a very early age of both the nobility and the fragility of the human being. The distance between the two traits is not that great. People can rise up to do extraordinary things. And they can fall far and fast.

A hospital, particularly a military hospital full of badly damaged people, tends to focus one on our similarities rather than our differences, on our shared needs and vulnerabilities. Scratch us and we all do bleed.

The Jesuit priest and distinguished paleontologist Teilhard de Chardin noted that "no evolutionary future awaits man except in association with all other men." I agree. Therefore, it not only behooves us to treat our fellow human beings with compassion and respect, it is essential for our collective survival. Unethical men and women can flourish for periods, sometimes very long periods, but ultimately their lack of morality—and their lack of humility—destroys them. You cannot build a strong and lasting business on a rotten foundation.

I was proud of the fact that The Coca-Cola Company always had a corporate culture founded on trust and the absolute necessity of doing the right thing.

I vividly remember when NBC ran a documentary back in the 1970s on the plight of migrant workers. We were utterly appalled to see that many of these people, hired by third-party labor contractors, were at work in our Minute Maid groves in Florida, some living in dreadful conditions. Paul Austin, our CEO at the time, sent our president, Luke Smith, and several others, including me, down to investigate. Conditions in many instances were indeed deplorable. Austin went before the Senate committee investigating the issue and when he was presented with some descriptions of the workers' situation, he not only acknowledged them, he said, "Senator, not only are conditions as bad as you say—they are worse than you can imagine. The Coca-Cola Company cannot, in good conscience, tolerate this situation. We are going to do a great deal to try to fix this."

And we did. Based on our findings we came up with a plan to upgrade the total standard of living for the workers. Our first instinct was to provide the workers with physical things such as better housing, better transportation to the groves, gloves for picking, ice water servers in the groves, and other amenities. Old housing was bulldozed. But our second thought was that simple welfare was not enough. Accordingly, we sent a team of behavioral scientists to Florida to plan a comprehensive program that would face up to the basic human problems involved. As a result of their study, the company opened a clinic and established social service centers offering child care, preschool training, and adult education. In addition wages and insurance benefits were increased. And community organizations were established, governed by the workers.

The farm workers union arrived and despite some initial unrest we managed to settle the issues amicably and from that point on, until most of the groves were sold or converted to other uses, our relationship with the migrant workers was positive.

As Austin said, we just could not, as a matter of conscience, tolerate the terrible circumstances of the migrant workers. It was not just public relations. It was the right thing to do.

To maintain public confidence in our capitalist system it must be managed by men and women of honor and decency. I am deeply troubled by the study at Rutgers indicating that of all graduate students, MBA students are the most likely to cheat. Recently it was reported that a number of MBA programs are beginning to touch on ethics issues and organize courses with "Business Ethics" in their titles. I hope they are successful. Yet if such courses are taught by faculty members who typically have no practical experience in the business world, the efforts will be less than effective. The real world is where you must decide ethical issues on a daily basis.

My father certainly needed no such ethics course. He was raised with the midwestern value that your word is your bond, and a man's handshake is as good as all the contracts in lawyerdom. My father would have agreed with Peter Drucker that there is no such thing as business ethics. Just *ethics*. It's not separate from the rest of your life. If you have a Rolodex of ethics or values for various circumstances, you're not a business person. You're Tony Soprano!

My father always said that he slept very well. I suspect the old adage is true—"A quiet conscience sleeps in thunder."

## Commandment Six

# Don't Take Time to Think

> *"The real problem is not whether machines think but whether men do."*
> —Burrhus Frederic Skinner

WE ARE A technologically obsessed society, and, on balance, that's a good thing because genuine and often remarkable improvements are made. The tinkerers of the past, like Edison, gave us the lightbulb and the tinkerers of today are giving us unbelievable computer capabilities. Richard Demillo, dean of the college of computing at Georgia Tech, says that we are in a whole new age of innovation. The world continues to change so that I can state with some confidence that most of the technical references in this book are already out of date.

Nevertheless, doing something with technology just because we *can* do it doesn't necessarily mean that we *should* do it. We frequently add to the complexity of life without gaining any discernible advantage—in fact, at times there are definite disadvantages. My car, for example, comes with a 712-page manual. It has a radio with so many controls and settings that it is difficult to turn it on and equally as difficult to turn it off. That's certainly counterproductive. My dream car radio has two buttons. One turns it on and adjusts the volume. The other button, when you simply turn it, in a nanosecond the broadcast changes to another station. If you turn it a bit more, it brings you another station. And so on. We are, I fear, however, a long way from such an advanced development.

Of course, there is no area where technology has so thoroughly enthralled us than in the field of communications.

We have kilobytes, megabytes, gigabytes, terabytes, petabytes, exabytes, zettabytes, yottabytes—the bytes just keep adding up, don't they? And to what end?

"More information" is the answer. In fact, it's been said that we live in the information age.

That's not true. We live in the *data* age. Data are coming to us endlessly, 24/7. More and more data coming at us, faster and faster, from all sides. According to one estimate, more than sixty billion e-mails are sent around the world every day. By the time you read this, the estimates will be in the trillions. Not to mention telephone calls, which are now in such stratospheric numbers that any guess as to the volume is meaningless.

We communicate and communicate—responding instantly like automatons pouring out a stream of consciousness that just adds more data to the flow—without any evaluation, without anyone really sitting back, shutting the door, turning off all the bells and whistles and in a few moments of quiet reflection doing some serious thinking.

In *Brave New World*, published in 1932, Aldous Huxley wrote, "People are never alone now. . . . We make them hate solitude, and we arrange their lives so that it's impossible for them ever to have it."

One of the great fears many businesspeople had in 2006 and 2007 was not fear of market failure or something catastrophic like that. It was the fear that maybe BlackBerry would go away. We're in danger of becoming a nation of squint-eyed hunchbacks because everyone is scrunched around these tiny little gadgets getting news of something, anything, everything.

I don't have any idea what the ultimate impact of the Internet-based social network services like MySpace and Facebook will be. It may be very positive. I hope it is. As we continue, however, to transform the nature of human interaction, we come very close to electronic sensory overload coupled with human sensory deprivation. The simple interaction of one human being with another is being lost. Even among children. When a large percentage of young people play, they don't just play, of course. Their lives are so structured that they have scheduled playdates—like business appointments. But when they are together, they often are not looking at each other. They look at screens or fiddle with little handheld things.

One magazine ad for Panasonic showed a man sitting in a car, typing away on a laptop with the copy: "It's not just a laptop. It's having your driver circle the building a few more times while you send a few more e-mails."

Can you imagine what it must be like working for this man? Thank goodness he's the fictional creation of Panasonic's advertising agency.

There are three major problems inherent in this addiction to all this unprocessed data flooding in without any time to think.

## 1. In-box Shock—the Human Toll

Many office workers are already showing symptoms of and complaining about what some have labeled "In-box Shock." There's just too much stuff to mentally sort. According to a study in 2006 the average corporate worker has to deal with 133 e-mails every day. Not only that, they deal with multiple communications—a fax here, a text message there—attend a meeting here and teleconference with another meeting there—watch a PowerPoint presentation here, watch a video report there. Phones ringing on the desk and vibrating in the pocket. The average human nervous system is not built to process material at anything approaching this blinding rate of speed and volume.

On Bloomberg TV the other day twelve headlines zipped by between 4:34 and 4:35 P.M. In addition, there were two crawls, a box score of the market indicators, and a continuous live commentary. That goes on all day. Every day. Endless words floating by, endless chatter, endless noise.

A Canadian study of academics at universities across that country indicated 42 percent said they felt stressed by the constant barrage of information and communication coming their way; 58 percent said their ability to stay focused on their work had greatly diminished due to ICTs (information and communication technologies). Also, doctors from a number of medical schools are reporting that because people tend to talk louder on phones in order to "animate" their conversations, vocal strain and subsequent hoarseness are becoming a growing problem.

Obviously, there are some people who seem to be able to handle all this, mentally and physically. They even thrive and grow rich on it.

A *Fortune* magazine article sometime back reported that Microsoft chairman Bill Gates has three monitors on his desk, synchronized so that he can drag items from one to another. One screen displays e-mail. The second screen shows the particular message that he is writing at that moment. The third screen is for a browser so he can search various sites.

Bill Gates is a pioneer of electronic communication. He is a genius, and especially a genius in the field of handling data. No one can measure the positive impact he has had on our global society. But for certain, he has brought us closer together . . . just a click away.

But for many of us mere mortals, however, ICTs far from freeing up time to actually focus on and think about what we are doing have frequently compressed time to stressful levels. The Dutch sociologist Ida Sabelis uses the word "decompress," which is what divers have to do when they surface after very deep dives. After we dive deeply into all kinds of data, we definitely need time to decompress, to sit back and think deeply about the issues before us.

It's said, "You can never have too much data." But instinctively, you and I know that simply is not true. If you have ever been pulled up short in the toothpaste department of your local drugstore, you know the problem: Colgate alone has fifteen or sixteen different varieties, all, apparently, providing some slightly different type of teeth cleaning, teeth whitening, and cavity prevention. That's just too much data to process.

Even more daunting, consider the process of buying something a bit technical, such as a new phone or a TV set. The choices are wonderful and totally mind boggling—for some of us, anyway.

Do you want a phone that takes pictures, stores music, surfs the Internet, sends and receives text messages, or displays the latest soap opera? All you need to know is there. Just go to any one of thousands of Web sites or talk to the friendly technologists at one of the many electronics retailers. There's so much to know, it can be difficult. (Smart salespeople know this, so they quickly try to narrow down your selection. Show me a dozen ties and I'm confused. Show me three and I usually pick the blue one.)

In the early 1970s a psychologist gave horse-racing handicappers varying amounts of information on various horses—past racing records, the weight they carried, breeding, and so on. Interestingly, the handicappers did worse on their predictions when they had forty pieces of information than when they had only five. It's true that in many, many situations less *is* more!

A global network of everything connected to everything already exists. Machines are constantly talking to machines. Groups are connected to groups, all sharing data. To be productive, however, the whole vast array needs structure. A business network may not have some kind of tangible structure, like a building, but at some point there must be some kind of guidance to keep the flow going in the right direction, toward the right goals.

Someone or some few people must actually apply wisdom and thought about the direction and goals.

Someone must have a vision of the future. The data alone do not get you there. In fact the data are often conflicting because a group consensus is altogether different from an individual decision. In a national poll people will happily *say* they want a more energy-efficient house, yet they will just as happily go out and build one three times the size they have now.

I believe in research, but I don't expect the research to give me much more than a glimmer, an imperfect snapshot, of a moment in time. Bell-shaped curves won't really tell me how to design a vision for the future. Surveys won't reveal how the dreams of tomorrow should be shaped because nobody knows. If the builders of early automobiles had asked people what they wanted in transportation, the probable answer would have been, "Faster horses."

If you want to fail, don't take time to think. If you want to succeed, take lots of time to think. Thinking is the best investment you'll ever make in your company, in your own career, in your life.

When Steve Bennett, a bright Jack Welch GE alum, took over as CEO of Intuit, the company had a set of ten operating values. He changed only one word in all ten values. The ninth one was "Think Fast, Act Fast." He changed it to "Think *Smart*, Act Fast." Intuit was doing well. It has done even better under Bennett's leadership. Taking time to think really matters. As Gandhi noted, "There is more to life than increasing its speed." Success is not all about moving faster. Failure, though, definitely is.

## 2. Data, Unprocessed, Can Mask Reality

In the early part of the twentieth century, traditional physics was being revolutionized by further advancements in quantum mechanics. You don't have to understand physics to have a grasp of the fundamental philosophical revelation that it is simply *impossible to know everything about the world*. The Heisenberg uncertainty principle ensures that we cannot be certain of what we observe because what we observe is influenced by the very process of observing. Not long ago a couple of physicists observed that we can't be too certain of the uncertainty principle, either!

So when we say we "know" something we'd best be cautious in our epistemological assertions.

---

*"It ain't so much the things we know that get us into trouble. It's the things we know that just ain't so."*
—Mark Twain

(Some *know* it was not Mark Twain who said this. It was Artemus Ward, Ralph Waldo Emerson, or Will Rogers. I *know*, for a fact, that it was none of these. It was my uncle Vern. I *know*. I was there when he said it.)

SOMETIMES WE SEE what we expect to see, not reality but the data that we think represent reality. Or that we want to represent reality.

There is a psychological bias called the confirmation trap. We seek to confirm our preconceived views rather than see what might be wrong with those views.

Enron fooled many people, including many in the firm itself. Yet Enron people were bamboozled simply because they did not really think about what they were looking at in the balance sheets. They were so eager for the implausible and incomprehensible numbers to be true that they ignored them. The business press was equally gullible. They wanted the "hot" story, not necessarily the truth. Again and again, art forgers and con artists of all stripes exploit the gullibility of even the most sophisticated among us. They understand our need to at times believe fantasy over reality.

In the late 1940s, when Pepsi was selling "twice as much for a nickel," Coca-Cola executives fooled themselves by quarterly reporting sales of the product in cases. And those case sales reports showed that Coke was selling far more cases than the competitor. The only problem was that a case of Coca-Cola was twenty-four six-and-a-half-ounce bottles while the case of Pepsi was twenty-four twelve-ounce bottles. No one asked the obvious question, "If we are selling more cases, why are they constantly gaining on us?" The reality of that question led to the final breakthrough of larger-size bottles for Coca-Cola.

Detroit automakers fooled themselves for years looking at the sales figures they wanted to look at rather than thinking about the total picture of the global automotive industry. They even fooled themselves on their standards of quality. They set their own internal standards, assigned their own value to a measure of quality, and then patted themselves on the back when they came *close* to their *own* standards. The Japanese had no standards. They said, "Let's build the best car we can. And let's keep improving that car." Obvious. And brilliant.

I've become very wary of all studies related to marketing and business management. They have their place, but I'm convinced that we are often measuring the wrong variables and the wrong people are evaluating the measurements.

The classic example for The Coca-Cola Company was the infamous introduction of New Coke in 1985. In blind taste tests that involved little sips of product A versus product B, the sweeter product won. This led us to the erroneous conclusion that Coca-Cola was not sweet enough.

But blind taste tests completely failed to portray the full dimensionality of the product Coca-Cola—its total image and cultural context.

In the United States, Pepsi sales were increasing at

the time, so the Coca-Cola leadership, and particularly leaders of the bottler community, were looking for reasons why Pepsi sales were doing a bit better than ours in supermarkets. And U.S. Coca-Cola management began looking for reasons. It was not advertising expenditures or distribution issues, so the problem had to be something else. That led them to focus on the nearly one-hundred-year-old product itself. Researchers asked the question: Was there some specific difference that could be pinpointed and corrected? And so two hundred thousand taste tests were conducted and proved beyond a doubt that it was a sweetness issue. It turned out that sweetness, of course, was not the problem at all. The data masked the reality. All the research in the world doesn't mean anything if you aren't asking the right questions. The reality was that there needed to be more intense excitement in the iconic brand. New Coke, in its own way, helped to do that, but it was a painful lesson.

Budget planning also suffers from too much data. Through the years, budget specialists in the Atlanta headquarters of Coca-Cola often drowned themselves in raw data that were next to useless, yet they kept collecting them and refining them according to some internal formula. For example, "The fountain sales department spent X dollars last year on in-store merchandising. Therefore, the department will require X plus Y next year, and we will plan accordingly!" Budget planners never really saw the whole picture.

In the late 1960s and early 1970s a few of us moved to Atlanta from the recently formed Coca-Cola Foods Division in Houston. Our advantage was that we were from out of town. We saw things through different lenses and began to put together a bigger picture. We had some mental distance from issues and took some time to think about the entire operation.

We saw the same furniture everyone else did, but we knew the sofa could be moved.

## 3. Not Taking Time to Think Is Just Plain Foolish—Even Dangerous

> " 'Forward the Light Brigade!'
> Was there a man dismayed?
> Not though the soldiers knew
> Someone had blundered:
> Theirs not to make reply,
> Theirs not to reason why,
> Theirs but to do and die:
> Into the Valley of Death
> Rode the six hundred."
> —Alfred Lord Tennyson

THE LIGHT BRIGADE went charging into the Valley of Death because its leaders just didn't pause to think. And all the soldiers blindly followed. Soldiers were not supposed to think for themselves, but their leaders were. It's obvious, but worth noting—one cannot make any real progress in any field, war included, if one just keeps sifting through data and reaches quick conclusions based on previous experience rather than careful evaluation and slow, careful analysis.

Time to think is not a luxury. It is a necessity. As Goethe noted: "Action is easy; thought is hard." Yet action frequently—in fact, more often than not—takes on a life of its own. We pay homage to reason, but we are held hostage to emotion. We are, after all, feeling creatures, and in the excitement of a particular endeavor once the ball is rolling, it's difficult to stop. There is a tendency toward group wishing in decision making wherein everyone is so eager to make something happen that straight thinking becomes almost impossible.

In the field of mergers and acquisitions, multimillion even billion-dollar deals get under way and the momentum builds, the rivalries among the players come to the fore, the game—and a game it becomes—goes ahead, no holds barred. Someone is determined to win! They can taste it! All the cash lying on the table, all the supposedly solid rationale behind the deal, all the people involved—nothing matters except winning! "I want my way," says the biggest ego in the room! There are dreams of being in the press conference spotlight and big headlines in the *Wall Street Journal*. It's all too glamorous and we convince ourselves that the numbers do add up—even when they are about as sound as astrological predictions. The "animal spirits" that John Maynard Keynes wrote of are more powerful than most business-people would like to admit.

Look at the recent dreadful fits—Daimler and Chrysler, Time Warner and AOL, Kmart and Sears, Quaker Oats and Snapple. Should these really have ever happened? The less than satisfactory results were wholly predictable, but people were swept up in the deal, and no one, top to bottom, thought through the consequences or the consequences of the consequences. Certainly, the short-term gain to various players is always going to be a factor, but there must be someone projecting ahead to the long-term consequences for the welfare and dignity of all the stakeholders in every business activity.

Unless somebody stops to think . . . it's easy to make the same mistakes over and over. And that is a sure pre-scription for failure. When there is a failure of some kind, begin looking around to assign blame or make ex-cuses or punish somebody. That way you won't step back to take the time to really analyze the failure. Good hos-pitals regularly convene morbidity and mortality ses-sions to discuss and learn from their own failures. Their cases involve life and death. Most businesses are not dealing with anything nearly so serious. But every mis-take provides a real opportunity to think about a less than successful technical change or a marketing faux pas and figure out, as objectively as possible, what went wrong.

Any management that is really doing its job is going to stumble from time to time. But if you want to fail, avoid looking closely at each mistake and don't analyze it. That way you will continue to make the same kind of mistake in the future.

If you still are determined to fail, however, it's imperative that you don't take time to think. Or, and this is really seductive, you can actually avoid almost all responsibility by getting someone else to do your thinking for you. This brings us to . . .

## Commandment Seven

# Put All Your Faith in Experts and Outside Consultants

> *"It is better to know some of the questions than all of the answers."*
> —James Thurber

IN MY TEENS, while working during the summer at the Sioux City stockyards, I became acquainted with a number of cattle buyers and sellers. One day one of them asked me to help him by becoming a bull buyer. Bulls were shipped in one at a time and were scattered across the complex. When bulls outlived their reproductive usefulness, they were sold for slaughter. But for most buyers it wasn't profitable to spend the time needed to wander all over the yards in order to buy one bull here and one bull there. However, an energetic summer student willing to go around and purchase fifteen or twenty bulls a day to fill a railcar could earn a fairly tidy commission, like twenty dollars or so.

I became a summer bull buyer for Doyle Harmon, the uncle of the famous Michigan football player Tommy Harmon. After my first day on the job, he came by and asked to see what I'd bought. It turned out I'd paid too much for quite a few of the bulls. Harmon reminded me that I was among salesmen and because of my young age, they would try to flatter me, be nice to me, distract me, but he pulled out a chart and said here's exactly what you are looking for in a bull. No matter what anyone says, never deviate from these basic requirements of conformation. He said, "Watch the bull, not the man."

That simple advice has stuck with me through my years in business even to this day in the world of investment banking. I always tried to separate the product from the presentation. That may seem like it would be easy, but it's not. No matter how sophisticated you might think you are, if you allow yourself to take your eyes off the bull for a moment and concentrate instead on the man, you can get drawn into the most preposterous ventures. In Commandment Six, I said you will fail if you don't stop to think. Well, you'll also fail big time if you let yourself be flattered, and there is never a shortage of charming con artists in just about every field who will use flattery as a sales tool.

It's a bit unfair of me to call them con artists. Most are quite sincere in what they're offering, whether it's marketing expertise or management strategies or the prospects for a new venture. They often have high qualifications and pose as absolute authorities. And they come heavily armed with definitive answers that can be boiled down into flashy PowerPoint presentations. The problem with many of their answers is that they address the wrong questions.

"Watch the bull, not the man" is good advice for those who are regularly exposed to fancy management-consulting presentations.

At Coca-Cola over the years, a parade of self-styled experts came and went both as inside employees and outside consultants, and sometimes we let them persuade us to do things that our better judgment, our gut instincts, warned us not to do—but like all fallible human beings, we had a weak moment or two.

For a number of years consultants had been telling the leaders of The Coca-Cola Company that it needed to diversify. The core business of soft drinks and juices gave us no hedge against the future and the company needed to look around to acquire businesses that were compatible but different. And the consultants had a number of recommendations. One of them was a very nice wine company. So listening to the consultants, the company acquired the wine business.

There was no question that the wine business was charming. It had a fine group of managers and they operated a separate unit called the Wine Spectrum. Management enjoyed having the bottles gracing the tables at our various corporate dinners and cocktail parties. The Wine Spectrum didn't get much real attention from the senior management of The Coca-Cola Company. It was sort of like owning a pet.

By that time, Robert Woodruff, well into his eighties, was still a great influence but not active in the day-to-day business. He decided, however, to take a personal look at this wine business "his" company had gotten into. (To his dying day, Mr. Woodruff always regarded Coca-Cola as "his" company.)

So the revered gentleman gathered his doctor and a few friends and took a company plane out to California. When he got back he had lunch with then CEO Roberto Goizueta and me. And as I remember his remarks, they went like this:

> Well, the wine business is interesting. I went out to California to see the vineyards.
>
> It seems that it takes five or six years for a vine to be mature enough before you can start harvesting grapes. During those years you've got quite a few people tending to the vines and praying for the right kind of weather so they yield a good crop. Finally, though, if everything works out, they pick the grapes and they take them to the plant where they squeeze them and put them into these great, hugely expensive stainless-steel tanks where they ferment. From these expensive tanks the wine goes into many small casks made out of equally expensive French oak. The casks cost fifty-five dollars each. The wine then ages for some time in the many small expensive casks.

Meanwhile, about 15 percent of the wine is lost through evaporation.

Soon, however, after aging quite awhile, the wine goes into bottles. They pay a tax at that time on each bottle and then put the bottles away for more aging. You keep the bottles for years, and if everything has gone well during the process and you have a reasonably good vintage, then you finally send the bottles into retail stores where there are hundreds of different kinds of wines on the shelves. At that point, you hope to God that out of that whole array of similar bottles someone is going to buy yours.

Now I grew up in a business where you bottle it in the morning and sell it in the afternoon and in a lot of places there is no other competition. Seems to me that's the kind of business we want to be in!

Mr. Woodruff struck a chord with Roberto and me. Despite what all the consultants had said about how good this business was, and despite the fact that we had acquired about 11 percent of the total U.S. wine business—a not insignificant share—we decided to take a closer look at the business. So we met with the managers of the Wine Spectrum in early 1981 shortly after we had taken our assignments to lead the company.

We asked wine executives to make the assumption

that every business decision they would make between then and 1990 would be perfect. We asked those executives to use volume and profit projections that were generous but rational and report what the expected return on invested capital would be by 1990. When we received that information the decision would be made on whether to build the business or get out of it. We assured the executives that they would have a place in the company should we sell the wine business.

Every one of those wine executives concluded that with the very best possible results, the return on capital would be equal to or less than our cost of capital. That gave us pause. Did we really want to be in this business?

But what could we do with it?

It always pays to be lucky and The Coca-Cola Company has been lucky over the years. Shortly after we concluded that we didn't really know how we could make a decent return in the wine business, a call came from Seagram's. They were interested in looking at our Wine Spectrum. And "reluctantly" we negotiated a deal that worked out very nicely for both parties.

Take your eyes off the bull and you will fail. I did.

When the management of Coca-Cola USA came to corporate leadership with a New Coke proposal, we were persuaded to take a serious look. This was a case where Roberto and I allowed ourselves to be convinced by consultants and experts that the huge number of taste tests conducted by the U.S. market research group provided us with a valid basis to make the move to an entirely new product formulation. After weeks of reviews, debate, and discussion, Roberto and I supported the project. They had convinced us that changing the product would be a brilliant competitive move.

Out it came. More testing. More experts. The company had focus groups and test markets and random samples. Everything clearly pointed to New Coke as always the winner. Roberto's and my gut instincts were not to mess with this icon of America's heritage, but the expert evidence was overwhelming. And the decision-making process began to be an exercise in what I referred to before as group wishing. It becomes, like it or not, a team decision because the idea is so exciting and seems so right to so many. New Coke was gathering so much momentum that no one on the team wanted to be the one to rain on the parade. Despite reservations, Roberto and I also were caught up in the gathering tidal wave propelling this dramatic change. We bought into the project 100 percent. For those of us who were part of this seismic event, the emotionally charged anticipation was palpable.

The company rolled out New Coke across the nation in April and May of 1985. To feed the frenzy, we put marching bands and balloons and everything else in our promotional bag of tricks behind the launch of New Coke.

It created quite a stir. In the historical scope of the world, it doesn't seem all that important, but at the time it was definitely a global news event.

Almost immediately after the announcement, complaints tied up the phone circuits to Atlanta in ever-increasing numbers of telephone calls. In a matter of a few weeks we had more than four hundred thousand letters and calls—all negative. Our experts urged us to stay the course.

One letter was from a lawyer in Idaho addressed to Roberto and me: "Gentlemen, will the two of you please autograph the bottom of this letter because it will soon be worth a fortune. It will bear the names of the two dumbest executives in American business history." A letter like that is good for one's humility curve.

Protesters were massing as far away as Seattle, where an organization called the Old Coke Drinkers of America had drawn five thousand people to their demonstration against New Coke. On the *Tonight Show*, Johnny Carson announced that there were now plans to change Twinkies and add spinach filling.

Some of our U.S. bottlers, who had been the most enthusiastic about the change, were telling us they couldn't play golf anymore because they were being accosted at their local clubs by fellow members who were angry over New Coke. Bottler salespeople were refusing to go into stores because they were being verbally attacked. People were driving pickup trucks to supermarkets and stocking up on old Coke. It was mass hysteria.

Our research gurus and marketing experts told us it was just a matter of time. New Coke was going to be a smash success. All the complaints are just keeping the Coke name in the press.

In late July, Roberto and I and our wives were in a small Italian restaurant just outside of Monaco following a meeting with the twenty-five largest Coca-Cola bottlers in the world. The proprietor had been told we were associated with The Coca-Cola Company and after we were seated, he approached the table carrying a wicker basket covered with a red velvet cloth, reserved for the finest table wines. He lifted the cloth and there was a bottle of Coca-Cola. "This is the real Coke," he proudly announced in broken English, like it was rare old cognac. Despite all the free publicity Coke was getting, that moment really caught our attention.

But it was an eighty-five-year-old woman who convinced me we had to do something more than stay the course. She had called the company in tears from a retirement home in Covina, California. I happened to be visiting the call center and took the call. "You've taken away my Coke," she sobbed.

"When was the last time you had a Coke?" I asked.

"Oh, I don't know. About twenty, twenty-five years ago."

"Then why are you so upset?" I asked.

"Young man, you are playing around with my youth and you should stop it right now. Don't you have any idea what Coke means to me?"

It became crystal clear that we were not dealing with a taste issue or any real marketing issue. All the experts and all their data had been misleading. This was a deep psychological issue. A brand is not defined by what *you* or I think it is. A brand is defined by what is embedded in the mind of each consumer. Because Coca-Cola is consumed by so many individuals in so many cultures, it is defined differently by every person.

The upshot was that I knew we could spend a fortune and we would never succeed in making U.S. entry of New Coke successful. Roberto also came to that same conclusion. The U.S. consumer had spoken clearly and loudly: Coca-Cola was their product and they wanted it back. We agreed. I went on TV and announced that we would be bringing back old Coke as "Coca-Cola Classic." Peter Jennings interrupted ABC's highly watched *General Hospital* with the breaking news that Coca-Cola was bringing back the original formula. Every major network and station covered it as the lead story on their newscasts. Newspapers ran banner headlines.

America went crazy. We got flowers and love letters. The whole thing ended like a classic Frank Capra motion picture. Big company makes a decision, the people rebel, the company backs down, and the people win. Consumers got their Coca-Cola and sales went through the roof. The consumers not only forgave us for our mistake; they adored us. Politicians might take a lesson from this incident. It pays to admit that you made a mistake, to admit that you are not infallible. The American people are very forgiving.

Meanwhile, the experts who helped us into this situation went on their way to "help" other people.

Whatever happened to common sense? The expertise of some experts has been disproved so many times that you would think they would wear out their welcome.

Philip Tetlock has been monitoring *experts'* views on world politics for many years. He notes, "Almost as many experts as not thought that the Soviet Communist Party would remain firmly in the saddle of power in 1993, that Canada was doomed by 1997, that neofascism would prevail in Pretoria by 1994, that EMU would collapse by 1997 . . . that the Persian Gulf Crisis would be resolved peacefully."* He found that these experts were 80 percent confident of their predictions. They were actually correct only 45 percent of the time. They might as well have been flipping coins.

But what was most telling was that in following up with these experts, despite incontrovertible evidence

*Philip Tetlock, "Theory-Driven Reasoning About Plausible Pasts and Probable Futures in World Politics," in Thomas Gilovich, Dale Griffin, and Daniel Kahneman, *Heuristics and Biases: The Psychology of Intuitive Judgment* (New York: Cambridge University Press, 2002).

that they had been wrong, Tetlock found that they showed no sign of losing faith in their own understanding of the situation. Instead, they manufactured a whole series of excuses—"I was almost right—it hasn't happened yet but it will—completely unforeseeable forces intervened like an earthquake—based on the data I was given, I was right."

> *It's October and an Indian chief believes it's going to be a cold winter. So he tells his tribe to collect firewood. To double-check his prediction, the chief calls the National Weather Service and asks a meteorologist if the winter is going to be a cold one. The weatherman says, "According to our indicators, we think it might." So the chief tells his people to find extra wood just in case. A week later he calls the National Weather Service again, and they confirm that a harsh winter is headed their way. The chief orders all his people to scavenge every scrap of wood they can find. Two weeks later, the chief calls the National Weather Service again and asks, "Are you sure this winter is going to be cold?" "Absolutely," the weatherman replies. "The Indians are collecting wood like crazy."*

THEY'RE WRONG, wrong, wrong again and again. Yet they keep coming around, prowling the halls of business and, yes, government, peddling some new expert observation, some prediction, some new jargon, or some new, recycled idea.

How many crazes can there be? Theory X. Theory Y. Chaos. Management by objectives. One-minute managing. Total quality management. Peak performance. Empowerment. Downsizing. Ramping up. Ramping down.

They are constantly "reengineering"—mainly they're reengineering the language. I recently heard one manager talk about "dehiring" some employees.

And what is matrix management? As near as I can determine, that means that thanks to the matrix, one person can enjoy the advantage of reporting to three, maybe more managers.

Just before the dot-com crash, I heard a lot about the term "burn rate." That's what we used to call simply spending someone else's money—money that they will never see again.

It's all rather amusing, except that our worshipping of experts can indeed lead to serious, and sometimes widespread, failure.

Consider John Meriwether and Long-Term Capital Management.

In the heady 1980s, Meriwether was among the headiest. He led a group of bond traders who generated profits for Salomon Brothers. In 1994, he and two others, economics Nobel Prize winners Myron Scholes and Robert Merton, founded Long-Term Capital Management, a highly unregulated investment pool in what is known as a hedge fund. Their clients were the extremely wealthy. Their brilliant theories were little understood but greatly admired because they could not fail! And for three years they delivered spectacular, almost unbelievable results. By 1998 they had invested some ninety billion dollars, most of it borrowed. But no one worried. The experts in charge knew what they were doing.

After the firm came tumbling down, the Federal Reserve Bank of New York intervened and organized a bailout among a hastily assembled consortium of creditors to prevent a disorderly collapse that could have affected trillions of dollars in contracts and shaken market confidence around the world.

The brilliant system the three men had devised and smoothly sold amounted to little more than a giant roulette game, but because people are so willing to put their faith in experts, their absurd scheme was accepted by some of the wisest men on Wall Street.

More recently, in 2007, we've seen financial markets in trouble because they were following statistical models that grossly underestimated how risky subprime lending could be. It was explained as "model error."

It wasn't model error. It was human error. Anybody with good gut feelings could have predicted that a lot of loans to people without any measurable means of repaying them was bad business. But the geniuses of the financial world kept planting their magic beans. And everybody was surprised when the money trees didn't grow. What folly!

The narrow perspective of what appears to be genius is often the inverse of wisdom.

This is especially true in the management of a large enterprise. Management is a craft, not a science. Beware of those who try to mathematize and quantify human behavior. We had managers and consultants at The Coca-Cola Company who saw people merely as numbers. They were not successful. You simply cannot put numbers on everything. It is, to my way of thinking, a failure of imagination.

During my lifetime I've also encountered many experts who try to evaluate a business *relative* to all the other businesses in that industry and come up with a plan to maximize profit based on industry averages. This is a terrible mistake because each company within an industry should be striving to differentiate itself, make itself in some way unique, not average. I never thought of Coca-Cola as *a* soft drink company. In my mind it was—and is—*The* Coca-Cola Company. The others are not "imitators," as my forebears in the company insisted. They just aren't selling Coca-Cola.

At the end of the day, after I've listened to all the marketing and financial geniuses who have paraded through my office, I find myself agreeing with the economist Ludwig von Mises: "Statistical figures . . . tell us what happened in a nonrepeatable historical case."

Of course, I must acknowledge that consultants and outside experts are often called on to simply validate a decision that has already been made by a manager insecure in his authority. I have always been fascinated by what happened at Chrysler after the death of its founder and leader, Walter P. Chrysler. Managers were so unsure of themselves that they held séances to try to get in touch with Chrysler to find out what the founder would have done. There is no evidence that they ever reached him. And had they been successful, he likely would have fired them all.

Managers involved in restructurings, common in the aftermath of mergers or in shrinking a business, often must confront the painful process of laying off employees. Rather than communicate in an honest and straightforward manner with the affected people, they sometimes try to place the blame on the new business plan designed by an outside consulting firm. I find this the height of cowardice. If you commissioned the new plan, it's your baby. You are responsible. In the end, if you are unwilling to assume responsibility, if you abrogate your authority to a third-party expert, you will not succeed in carrying out the new plan anyway.

I always made it a rule that no bad news, including firing people, could be delivered by e-mail or a memo or a telephone call. Any subject matter that carries strong psychological impact deserves face-to-face communication.

In his final letter to the General Electric stockholders Jack Welch advised, "Hate the bureaucracy in your organization." Therefore—my next commandment.

# Commandment Eight

## Love Your Bureaucracy

WHEN I FIRST came from Houston in 1973 into the Coca-Cola headquarters building in Atlanta as the new executive vice president, I found my longtime secretary, Florence Kalinowski, in tears. She had come in a few days ahead of me to set up the office. But she couldn't.

Why not?

She couldn't get any pencils.

In the smaller, more unstructured operation at the Food Division in Houston if she wanted pencils she just walked down to the supply room at the end of the hall. In Atlanta, she had to fill out some requisition forms, she was told, but she didn't have any requisition forms and as it was now late in the afternoon, the requisition form person had already left for the day. This was the last straw for Florence. She'd been fighting the headquarters bureaucracy for two whole days to get a copy machine set up, to get the phones hooked up, to get the stationery changed, to get a larger file cabinet—and so on and on until finally she snapped.

"I can't get anything done," she cried. "I can't even get staples for the stapler that *I* bought!"

I sent her home and called my wife, Mickie, to tell her I couldn't do any work that day, so we might as well have an early dinner and catch a movie.

If you want to get nothing done, make sure that administrative concerns take precedence over all others! Love your bureaucracy!

The word "bureaucracy" first popped up in French economic literature sometime in the mid-eighteenth century, from "bureau," *office*, and "cratic," *rule*. Many nineteenth- and early-twentieth-century political scientists and sociologists debated the pros and cons of bureaucracies. There were many cons, as you might expect. The Scottish curmudgeon Thomas Carlyle called bureaucracy "the Continental nuisance."

But there were those who recognized that bureaucracy was good, even necessary. Historically, it must have evolved quite logically from the heavy administrative requirements involved in carrying out any large enterprise.

In a primitive tribal society, we assume that leaders could simply come to the fore based on their own charismatic appeal. And much like Maori warriors, with enough fire in their eyes they could take charge as chieftains or warlords. However, as societies became more complex, charismatic leadership would not have been sufficient. Clearly, the Chinese could not have built their early empire, nor the Egyptians, nor the Romans without some form of bureaucratic organization. Even with slavery, brute force could not have attended to all the details.

Around the turn of the twentieth century, the German sociologist Max Weber pointed out that in large social organizations over time, hierarchical orders of authority were formalized; written rules, specialized training, and, most important, *offices* with titles and defined functions came into being.

The inventions of mankind that seem the most remarkable to me are those that we simply take for granted because, now that we have them, they seem so obvious. Who, thousands of years ago, came up with the idea of *money*, for instance? What a great idea—to take little bits of something (silver, gold, shells, beads) and then trade them for tangible assets. (I have some more to say about money later on.)

To me, the idea of the *office* in a bureaucracy is similarly brilliant.

Weber viewed bureaucratic systems rather bleakly as efficient but impersonal robotic machines. But in our modern society, with our many, many complex institutions, we would come to a grinding halt without such offices. In government and in every large business organization, we have office after office—the vice president of sales, the manager of distribution, the manager of human resources—all neatly laid out on a chart. Each office can be occupied over time by a series of people who carry out the duties of that particular office in order to attain the ongoing goals of the company. It's beautiful. The people change, but the function of the offices remains constant. We must have that capability in order to maintain continuity of authority.

I always said that any authority or influence I may have had in the world of Coca-Cola emanated from the word on my business card defining my *office:* "President." Not from my name at the bottom of the card. And the importance of the title resulted from the second name on the card: "The Coca-Cola Company." The least important name on the card was mine.

And I meant it.

But I also feel that the geometrically elegant machinery of the organization should not get in the way of the human creativity and productivity of individuals.

Personality—personal creativity—personal feelings—personal emotional commitment—personal imagination—there has to be room for these ineffable qualities in every job throughout an organization.

Leaders of complex organizations walk a fine line. They are not running a playroom. There must be rules and routines in every business to maintain the proper rhythm in everything. Over time, however, it seems that inevitably the rules and routines become more important than the ends they were designed to serve. The rules and routines become rigid, obsolete rituals and obstacles to the positive energy of the system.

The bureaucrats who control these rituals guard them with their lives because any change undermines their own power or authority. Gradually the bureaucrats themselves simply can and often do become a major impediment to progress of any kind and guarantee failure.

And do they keep busy! They churn out internal reports and memos. They cover their backsides with trails of thousands of e-mails and memos in the file. They go home at night complaining of how hard they work and in reality no single productive event has taken place all day. In such an enterprise failure is certain. According to the paper industry a few years ago, more than five hundred billion copies are made on office copy machines in the United States every year. And regarding last year's copy-machine output, the experts are still counting. What on earth is being copied by whom to whom about what? I thought e-mail would eliminate all the paper flow.

(Look at what Xerox really started!)

Having spent my very early years around my father's cattle business, it was clear that if you kept the right mix of male and female animals you would end up with a lot more animals. Bureaucracies multiply in the same way. Here's how it works: You put a manager in place and within eighteen months he or she has an assistant. The assistant becomes a junior manager and guess what? Another assistant. The beat goes on.

There are layers upon layers of people, yet when a customer calls, nobody's home. They are all in meetings. These meetings generate more paperwork, more e-mails, more calls, more meetings. In fact, most often there are even meetings to plan meetings. Meetings are the religious services of a great bureaucracy and the bureaucrats are fervently religious.

In my days at the Coca-Cola Foods Division in Houston, we didn't have much of a bureaucracy. We were a young company created by the merger of Duncan Foods and Minute Maid. Charles Duncan, who led the unit, was a tough, smart, frugal entrepreneur of Scottish roots. He abhorred bureaucracy and did everything to keep it under control. At the Foods Division we did not have five layers of management between the janitor and the president. We moved quickly and efficiently, and, I might add, profitably.

Later, Charles became president of The Coca-Cola Company and subsequently a cabinet officer in the Carter administration. When he asked me to join him in Atlanta in the U.S. soft drink operation he warned me that significant changes were needed to streamline the large, decades-old system at Coca-Cola headquarters. He was right.

Shortly after I arrived and discovered that the big

Coca-Cola bureaucracy had reduced Florence to tears over those unobtainable pencils, I began to learn another lesson about a large bureaucracy: They never say no. They just don't do what you want when you want.

After I had settled into the U.S.A. headquarters building I happened to notice that the small carpet in one of the elevators was tired and frayed. So I asked Florence to call the maintenance department and have the carpet replaced. Some months later, I mentioned to Florence that they hadn't gotten around to replacing that carpet. She said no, but they're doing a number of routine maintenance things, and it's on the schedule.

A year later when I became president of the division I mentioned that the carpet in the elevator hadn't been replaced yet. I was told it's on the agenda right now. When I moved from Coca-Cola USA to the corporate offices two years later the carpet in the elevator had still not been replaced. The maintenance department never refused our request. I never heard a "no." All we got, though, was no new carpet.

If you want to impede all real progress, make sure that administrative concerns take precedence over all others! Love your bureaucracy!

Every organization has choke points, another hallmark of an entrenched bureaucracy that no one, not even the top managers, is able to break through. And you dare not insult those keepers of the choke points or else they will drag their feet even more slowly in providing whatever service it is they are to supply. Some years ago when copy centers became the latest office innovation and all copies were made on a few centralized large copying machines, massive choke points began to impede efficient operations. In many cases, the person in charge of the process frequently became a stubborn tyrant, consumed with his or her own power and authority. Even to get the simplest, most routine order executed required endless flattery.

Similar situations exist in every department in a bureaucracy and these internal barons cannot be crossed. Going over the head of someone who runs the travel department or the office supply department in charge of paper clips will often result in vindictive behavior toward you later on. The result is that getting any service from them, even a ticket or a paper clip, becomes a personal battle. Not too long ago, in a column on such office tyrants, *Wall Street Journal* writer Jared Sandberg wrote of a particularly obstructive purchasing agent who demanded a requisition form for even the smallest item. When a secretary came to him because she had run out of requisition forms he told her: "Fill out a requisition form."

A sclerotic bureaucracy is frustrating because entrenched bureaucrats do little productive work themselves, but they clearly also prevent others from doing their work. Bureaucrats are so busy protecting their own turf that they will actually block the flow of essential information and subvert any opportunity for success in order to enhance their own.

The old law of the business jungle, "Your success is my failure," is fully operational in a heavily layered bureaucracy. You can almost smell the blood. Rivalry is a part of human nature. But more often, the more petty the issues and the more inconsequential the rivalry, the more counterproductive the struggle.

The whole institution is a Gulliver tied down by hundreds of Lilliputians. It's been said there is a new game called Bureaucracy. Everybody stands in a circle and the first person to do anything loses!

If you want to lose some of your best talent, make sure that administrative concerns take precedence over all others! Love your bureaucracy!

Human resource experts have told me that when you lose a middle-level manager, the cost of finding, attracting, and training a replacement will be at least two times the former employee's average annual salary. Clearly, it pays to hang on to good people. During my years at The Coca-Cola Company, we fought to keep our most talented people, as did most companies. In a far-flung global enterprise, some people inevitably will be lured away. But if we learned that an employee we valued was dissatisfied we would move quickly to find out why and try to turn the situation around. Sometimes the information did not arrive soon enough, and the person was lost before anything could be done. Sometimes nothing could be done.

But I learned from the experience that one of the reasons often given for an employee's leaving was not money, not the difficulty of the work. It was the bureaucracy! They couldn't get their work done. They were frustrated, but unlike the Coca-Cola manager in Japan who often threw away the memos and directives from headquarters, they didn't quite have the courage to do so.

In exit interviews, the answer to the question Why are you leaving? was often the stifling burden of bureaucracy.

One of the major challenges at any big company is always to eliminate unnecessary bureaucracy. As president of The Coca-Cola Company, I always described myself as a high-priced janitor. My job was to keep the aisles clear so that our brightest associates could get their jobs done, which was creating and serving customers and adding to shareholder value.

Very early in my business career I came to the not so startling conclusion that every business is mainly about serving present customers effectively and creating new ones. Whether your business is cars or cosmetics or computers, you're really in the customer business. Even if your business is something rather arcane, like putting out oil fires, you must market your expertise in the putting out of oil fires before anyone will even consider availing themselves of your special service. Red Adair, who did put out oil fires, marketed his reputation around the world so that his name—his "brand" name—became synonymous with this particular skill.

The Coca-Cola brand is synonymous with good feelings, pleasant times, refreshment. "Things go better with Coke," the advertising proclaimed, and while at the company, our job was to keep everyone and everything focused on making sure that every person with whom we came in contact would be convinced that things really did indeed go better with Coke. From the people who answered the phones to the men and women of the Coca-Cola bottler system to the chairman's office and even to the board of directors, while we all may *do* different things, our real job is marketing Coca-Cola.

The legendary story around the company was that once Mr. Woodruff and the company's general counsel were in a gathering of several people who were acquainted with both men. At one point Mr. Woodruff asked the lawyer to tell the group what his job was. Without a moment's hesitation, the general counsel responded, "Mr. Woodruff, I sell Coca-Cola."

That role was always at the top of my list of responsibilities. I encouraged strong sales-oriented thinking throughout the company and the entire Coca-Cola system worldwide. Every expense we made, every department we created, every project we took on had to answer the basic question: Will this help to create and serve customers? If the answer was not a ringing and positive "Yes!" whatever it was we were spending or undertaking had to be eliminated. Once you decide you have fifty things to do that are unrelated to your customer, soon you have fifty bureaucracies composed of individuals doing things extremely well that they shouldn't have been doing at all because it didn't serve the customer in any way.

Many companies lose their way. When they get off the ground they are lean and mean, watching cash flow and waiting until the mail comes in on Monday to see what they can spend on Tuesday. As they become successful, it's easy to become more casual and as a result they sow the seeds of failure. The sense of discipline slips. The breeding of assistants to assistants to assistants takes over and pretty soon there is a new reality. People are looking at one another, asking, "How on earth did we get this big? Who are all those people down the hall?" It happens.

Dell Computers started out as a very lean company. Over time they grew larger and larger with more and more layers of management. They became unprofitable and lost their number-one status to Hewlett-Packard. At that point, the founder, Michael Dell, stepped back in as CEO. One of the first things he did was to write an e-mail to all employees: "We have great people . . . but we also have a new enemy: bureaucracy, which costs us money and slows us down. We created it, we subjected our people to it and we have to fix it!"

It's axiomatic that bureaucracies will clash and work against one another. I worked very hard to minimize the friction by discouraging anyone from coming into my office to criticize another department. If there were any criticisms to be leveled, I wanted them aired in a room when everybody was looking at each other. I also tried to discourage people from giving me information or posing a question in the hallway. It's easy to get trapped into what I call management on the way to the bathroom!

You're on your way to the bathroom and someone buttonholes you, saying, "I've been meaning to talk to you about something." I always tried to steer them away by saying, "Wait until the operating meeting and then we'll talk about it." Most of the time, we were able to resolve differences, or at least control the potential damage.

Bureaucracy is a tough beast to tame.

> *"A committee is a group of men who individually can do nothing, but as a group decide that nothing can be done."*
> —Fred Allen

WARREN BUFFETT reported that in one of the companies Berkshire Hathaway took over, in the first month they eliminated fifty-four committees that were eating up about ten thousand man-hours monthly. As Buffett said, "It's unbelievable how much bureaucracy can build up in businesses, particularly those in which you can pass almost all of your costs to the consumer."

Just for the record, in 2007, Berkshire Hathaway owned more than 76 companies with almost 232,000 employees generating revenues of more than $18 billion. Their world headquarters staff consists of 19 people.

Peter Drucker spent more than sixty years teaching, consulting, and writing more than thirty books. One of his consistent themes was that smart enterprises don't micromanage their employees, ordering around every minute detail of their lives. Smart enterprises value their employees and encourage their contributions and encourage their creative spark. Dumb enterprises, by contrast, let layers of bureaucracy smother their employees' imaginations.

> *"What do you do, Bob?"*
> *"Nothing."*
> *"And what do you do, George?"*
> *"I'm his backup."*

DRUCKER'S ONGOING CRITICISM of bureaucracy culminated in a landmark article entitled "Sell the Mailroom," which ran in the *Wall Street Journal* in 1989 and was republished in 2005. At a time when the vast majority of businesses were busy trying to improve the efficiency of support staff, Drucker suggested that they should be eliminated entirely by outsourcing their work to independent contractors. Drucker noted:

> In-house service and support activities are de facto monopolies. They have little incentive to improve their productivity. There is, after all, no competition. In fact, they have considerable disincentive to improve their productivity. In the typical organization, business or government, the standard and prestige of an activity is judged by its size and budget—particularly in the case of activities that, like clerical, maintenance, and support work, do not make a direct and measurable contribution to the bottom line. To improve the productivity of such an activity is thus hardly the way to advancement and success.
>
> When in-house support staff are criticized for doing a poor job, their managers are likely to respond by hiring more people. An outside contractor knows that he will be tossed out and replaced by a better-performing competitor unless he improves quality and cuts costs.

Outsourcing to create a flatter, leaner organization is a more efficient and arguably more innovative way to run a business.

If you want to fail, love your bureaucracy—to death!

I have one final observation on the hazards of bureaucracy: At their worst, they cannot only impede success, they can also precipitate disaster.

On January 28, 1986, the space shuttle *Challenger* exploded shortly after liftoff, killing all seven of its crew members. On board was Christa McAuliffe, the first participant in the NASA Teacher in Space Program.

On February 1, 2003, the space shuttle *Columbia* burned up on reentry over Texas, killing all seven of its crew members.

Both of these disasters were attributed to technical flaws.

Because we don't have firsthand knowledge, we can only speculate based on information that came to light in the public hearings and in other postmission analysis. There are no doubt many who would argue otherwise, but a number of analysts seem to agree that the technical failures in these missions were partially the consequence of bureaucratic failure.* The decisions to launch both of these shuttles were made by a multilayered

---

*Jeff Forrest, "The Challenger Shuttle Disaster: A Failure in Decision Support System and Human Factors Management." Originally prepared November 26, 1996; published October 7, 2005, at URL DSSResources.COM.

NASA bureaucracy that was attempting to serve a multitude of masters—the scientific community, the Pentagon, the administration, and Congress. In addition, there were suppliers of parts and systems who were also a part of the decision-making process.

Anyone who has been a part of any emotionally laden decision knows how many forces can be at play, sometimes driving the most rational considerations to the sidelines. My decision-making experiences, especially with New Coke, lead me to believe that NASA might have faced similar, though, of course, vastly more critical problems in their decision-making process. As I said earlier, the greater the excitement, the greater the sense of urgency, and the more cooks there are in the kitchen, the greater the chance that bureaucratic decision making will either be deadlocked or the decision will become an exercise in group wishing. As was the case with New Coke, as is the case in certain mergers or acquisitions, no one on the team wants to rain on the parade!

And when there are many countervailing forces at play within a layered bureaucracy, turf battles can further compound the situation. Ultimately, a bureaucracy can become so dysfunctional that there is literally no one who *can* rain on the parade. The team can never make anything approaching an objective decision. Within NASA, the evidence appears to indicate that responsibilities were so diffuse that everyone evidently thought someone else in the system would catch an error. But it did not happen. From the testimonies after the disasters, it appears that the ultimate decisions to go were not made by those with the best information but by those with the most power.

The story of the Katrina disaster is a case study in dysfunctional bureaucracies. Books have and will continue to be written about the complete bureaucratic failures at every level, failures that created untold suffering and death.

When bureaucracies in business malfunction, it is difficult and costly. A lot of time is wasted sorting things out; therefore people are probably much more likely to make mistakes because of the sheer frustration just trying to get off the dime. But those kinds of mistakes just cost money.

When bureaucracies clash in major decisions of life and death the costs can be catastrophic. (Clearly, based on recent performances, NASA has ironed out its decision-making process and found a way to better harmonize its bureaucracies. The Federal Emergency Management Agency also has apparently streamlined its policies and procedures to remove layers of bureaucracy.)

# Commandment Nine

## Send Mixed Messages

> *"The problem with communication is
> the illusion that it has been accomplished."*
> —George Bernard Shaw

SENDING MIXED or confused messages to your employees or your customers will jeopardize your competitive position, and result in failure. Jack Welch has indicated that when he took over GE, the company was a jumble of mixed messages, with many longtime units on the brink of failure. At The Coca-Cola Company in the early 1970s, there were a number of situations where our communication was, at best, misleading, especially to our own people and our bottlers, but also to our retail customers. One troublesome situation was in our fountain department, where management had been sending several mixed messages.

*Like the parent who tells the child, "Clean your plate
or no dessert!" We said it, but we didn't mean it. They
got dessert anyway.*

When I came to Atlanta to work in our U.S. soft drink operations in 1973, the fountain department was the historic darling of the company. After all, it was at that soda fountain in Atlanta where Coca-Cola started and year after year we continued to roll along nicely, selling our products in cups or glasses through all kinds of outlets from McDonald's to Yankee Stadium. We had about seven hundred salespeople who called on these customers. A few served the chain accounts, calling at their headquarters level. The vast majority of the salespeople was out calling on individual retail outlets helping them to merchandise our products at the point of sale. There was no question that Coca-Cola was the leader in the fountain market around the world.

The problem was, well, there were several problems. Mainly, though, all of a sudden we were losing money!

To begin with in the late 1960s, the fountain department put a strange allocation system in place based on the salesperson's projection of what an outlet would sell in a calendar year. Most good salespeople are by their nature optimists. Now the issue was that the outlets received all of the promotional moneys at the beginning of the year based on the salesperson's projection. The problem showed up in December, when the fountain outlet's sales were dramatically less than the estimate.

One doesn't need to be a mathematician to determine that the company paid cash for sales that did not take place and gross margins disappeared. That in itself was a mixed message to the fountain outlet and to the company.

In addition to this rather bizarre arrangement, we kept absorbing the inflated costs of the ingredients in the syrup because it seemed to be etched in stone that the price of Coca-Cola syrup to the retail customer was fixed. Over the years costs had increased and margins narrowed, and the management at the time refused to deal with the issue, fearing that a price increase would jeopardize our business and make it vulnerable to a competitive attack. The truth was that while our costs were going up, so were our competitors' and I believed they could ill afford not to follow suit.

It was then that Charles Duncan asked me to come to Atlanta and work with the president of Coca-Cola USA, Luke Smith. My first assignment was to deal with this fountain department problem. After reviewing the situation, it became obvious that we had no alternative but to raise the price. One after another of the fountain department managers came to me and carefully explained that we could not raise prices. After listening to them, we still made the decision one Friday to raise the price about twenty cents a gallon.

The next Monday competition did not kill us. They raised their price too.

It just shows you how an idea can become so entrenched that it's immovable. My view from the outside was to look at the furniture a little bit differently from those who'd been living with it. I moved the sofa! And the house did not collapse.

I've mentioned the wonderful invention of money. Over my many years in business, I've thought a lot about how to recognize cash in real terms. Cash or money is the great abstraction that makes all commerce possible.

But I always used to worry that we were moving to such levels of abstraction in our company that we could no longer keep track of the score.

At the Foods Division in Houston in 1971, I realized that it was possible for people to graduate with a bachelor's degree or an MBA, go to work for the company, stay there forty years handling day-to-day operations, and never see a dollar in cash. Not a dollar in cash is paid to employees, to suppliers, to the media for advertising, to the ad agency itself, to the travel agents, and so on. In the headquarters, staff executives are just dealing with budgets that are nothing more than black-and-white numbers. It's very deceptive. It's so abstract that there is no meaning.

In Las Vegas they'll fire a croupier if money appears on a table and doesn't disappear in a second. They don't want people to think about real dollars and cents, so they use colorful chips. Gamblers will tip a fifty-dollar chip for a free drink because they aren't thinking "fifty dollars." They're thinking, "Just another little chip!"

The federal government spends about 7.4 billion

dollars a day. Yet a billion is a truly staggering number. A billion minutes ago, the Roman emperor Hadrian was building his wall. A billion hours ago, our ancestors were living in the Stone Age. A billion days ago, *Homo erectus* didn't exist.

A number of years ago C. Northcote Parkinson in his famous *Parkinson's Law* suggested that most people are not able to really comprehend just how much money is represented by all the little zeros on a large budget plan. They really only grasp much smaller sums, like a few hundred, or, at the most, several thousand. I had been thinking about ways to get the Foods Division employees to think about the real money they were spending, about every dollar that comes in and goes out. One year the thought came to me: "Let's not just *think* about real cash. Let's *use* cash!"

I called the chief financial officer and said that for the first week of next month, I want to do everything in real-cash-dollars-and-cents money. If an executive is taking a trip to New York and the ticket costs $692, I want him to plunk down $692. If a full-page ad in the *New York Times* is going to cost $19,458 dollars, I want the person responsible to lay out $19,458 in cash. I want to pay every bill in cash. Everything we touch. Cash for the salaries. Cash for the pencils. Cash for every single transaction.

The Foods Division wasn't a small business, but it

wasn't a corporate giant, either. Nevertheless, there wasn't enough available cash in all of the banks in Houston to carry out the experiment.

It was an outrageous idea, of course, and we never were able to do it. But it certainly would have been an interesting lesson to have people connect with real money instead of dealing with just numbers in budgets.

I was never able to effectively dramatize the hard reality of money, but with the fountain department I was at least able to drive home the importance of making some.

One final mixed message with the fountain department was that no matter how well or how poorly things were going, it was a long-standing tradition that every winter all the fountain department management and salesmen and -women and their spouses would gather for a "sales meeting," which was, in fact, a lavish celebration at some exotic sun-soaked watering hole. Sure enough, the year I arrived they were still planning the sales meeting, even though we were in the process of losing money.

Mixed message: "It doesn't matter what you do. You'll be rewarded."

So among the changes being planned, one of them was that the company was no longer going to reward poor performance. To make the point, I announced, "This year we're going to have the sales meeting in Chicago. Chicago is an exciting city, but not a resort in January. We'll meet at a commercial hotel. A rather second-tier hotel. No spouses. Everyone will stay two to a room."

I told them I didn't like the hotel, either. And I didn't like January in Chicago much more. But they couldn't spend money they didn't have.

They got the message.

The next year they had tremendous increases in sales and profits, and we had a big celebration in Hawaii. With spouses!

And they made money every year thereafter.

---

*"There are many things in life more important than money, and they all cost money."*
—Fred Allen, again

(He should have been teaching
at the Harvard Business School.)

---

MIXED MESSAGES could be the theme of one of my most harrowing experiences. In 1985, I was to receive the Martin Luther King Peace Prize from the Jamaican government. The prime minister, Edward Seaga, and a number of generals were there. During breakfast the generals kept whispering to the prime minister. Finally, he whispered to me, "After the speech you are not going out to the car. We're going up to your room." Which I did. As far as I could see in all directions there were fires burning and people shouting and chanting. I asked, "Has Coca-Cola done something here in Jamaica that I should know about?" "Oh, no. The people are just upset because gas prices have just gone up, but we don't want to take any chances." So they loaded me into a helicopter and off we went. It has always struck me as supremely ironic that we were there receiving the Peace Prize and we had to escape in a helicopter with machine gunners on the struts!

At The Coca-Cola Company, the greatest problem with mixed messages happened with our worldwide bottler system. Gradually, the system became out of sync with the world's retail system and major realignment was needed. The system simply had not kept up with the changes that had occurred in the social and economic fabric of the world.

Technology alone was responsible for much of the change. On July 10, 1962, a live television picture was transmitted across the Atlantic via the new communications satellite, Telstar. From that moment on, by leaps and bounds, the globe grew smaller and smaller.

One day it seemed that from country to country everybody in the world dressed a bit differently, sang different songs, read different publications, and watched different TV shows. The next day, it seemed, they all looked alike, played the same music, read the same things, and watched the same shows. From Bangor, Maine, to Bangalore in India, everybody was wearing Levi's, T-shirts, and sneakers. By the 1970s, rock 'n' roll and televised sports were bringing the world together as never before. Everyone everywhere knew Muhammad Ali. The 1976 Olympics were watched by more than a billion people. Even some of the same foods were being served everywhere.

As the world was becoming smaller and more "globalized," however, The Coca-Cola Company found itself sending increasingly discontinuous messages to our far-flung enterprise. We couldn't seem to get everyone around the world on the same marketing page, committed to the same overall goals. In a time when the world was becoming more one, we were not. "Coca-Cola" might well have been the second most recognized words in the world after "OK," but the company itself had markedly separate identities all over the world. And the seeds of failure were beginning to bear fruit.

The main reason was simply the way the system was built: Over many decades, the Coca-Cola international business was created by a group of company missionaries who were sent out to convert the world. They each saw that world through their own eyes and were, as I indicated earlier, pretty much on their own. They were given tremendous latitude because there really was no other way to build a great global business. As a result, the way the business was developed and the ways the product and the company were perceived in various parts of the globe were different. The only things that were not different were the taste of Coca-Cola, the trademark, the package, and the passion of the system and a great global business was built with this system. Those differences that did exist can frequently be traced directly to the man who originally carved out that corner of the earth.

For instance, one Coca-Cola pioneer named Bill Bekker went to Latin America. He found a world in which there were huge populations but low earning power. So he designed a business built around volume. He sold millions of cases of Coca-Cola at a price affordable to everyone from the Rio Grande to Patagonia. In that part of the world, then, we had a great *high-volume*, *low-margin business.*

In Europe, another pioneer named Max Keith was working with a much smaller population that had a higher income. Juices and all kinds of beverages were already a way of life in Europe, so he positioned Coke as a special treat, a special treat for special occasions. In that part of the world, we had a great *low-volume*, *high-margin business.*

Similarly, our business was organized and structured somewhat differently in each country in Asia, in Africa, in the Middle East. In some places we were supermodern and streamlined. In other places products were brought to market on donkeys. What we had was a wonderful mosaic made up of many separate baronies united around a common product and common quality standards, but different in so many other respects that the businesses could hardly talk to one another. And for many years, they really didn't need to.

## A Need for One Sight, One Sound, One Sell

But in the 1960s, the world was changing rapidly. Even faster in the 1970s. Markets were coming together, transcending borders. The marketing of Coca-Cola that had heretofore been merely suggested with certain pattern advertising provided by the Coca-Cola Export Corporation in New York was in need of new energizing that would dovetail with the global marketing efforts of global customers, such as McDonald's or hyperlarge supermarkets. We needed more availability of new packaging, such as cans and larger bottles. Plus, we were finding that while we had a series of separate companies running separate businesses, our consumers around the world were becoming more homogeneous in their tastes.

In the 1970s, then chairman and CEO Paul Austin moved the Export Corporation from New York to Atlanta, and to gain some global continuity, meetings with

Coca-Cola executives from around the world were more regularly scheduled. But once you have such a divergent culture, as we did, it's difficult to change it.

By the middle of the 1970s, when recession hit in the United States and inflation exploded and while we were renegotiating contracts with our domestic bottlers, political turmoil was affecting South America. Meanwhile, Europe and Asia were rapidly changing. At the same time, our principal competitor was granted an exclusive contract in Russia, and the Arabs wanted nothing to do with Coca-Cola because the company had granted a bottling franchise in Israel. The competitor's marketing was being revitalized. The Coca-Cola Company's stock price was way down. In short, the world of Coca-Cola was seriously unsettled.

## A Need to Shake Up the Old Order

In 1981, when Roberto Goizueta and I moved into the senior leadership positions of the company we faced a number of challenges. For instance, there was the immediate need to reinvigorate our image by introducing a product that we had known we needed for several years—Diet Coke. But our greatest challenge was to unify the direction and goals of the whole worldwide organization. It was risky to stir around and shake up some of these long-established fiefdoms, but we had to in order to modernize our marketing and gain efficiencies in our distribution system and to serve our global customers.

The first order of business was to unmix the mixed messages and convince everyone that while each sector of our global business could remain relatively autonomous, as markets had become more transnational, we needed to do likewise.

Red Auerbach, the legendary Boston Celtics coach, said that if a player missed a pass from another player it was the passer's fault because, as Auerbach put it, "if the passer was communicating properly, the receiver would get the message and be at the right place at the right time to catch the ball." The burden was on us to make sure every leader of the business from every part of the world would catch the message that our business—their business—had to change.

All the leaders of our business from around the globe participated in a meeting in Palm Springs, California. Roberto began the meeting with an astounding proposition, which he called "slaying a sacred cow every day." It was necessary to reinvent the company almost from the beginning, he said, and then we presented a clear, straightforward mission statement that we had worked on for some time. Fundamentally, we were consolidating the control of the international business in Atlanta with a single driving purpose while still maintaining the strengths and individuality of each local operation. We succeeded in implementing a "think-global, act-local" strategy long before it was fashionable.

## One More Mixed Message About What Business We Are Really In

I mentioned earlier the perceived need for Coca-Cola to diversify. In the case of the wine business, we found that promises of synergy were unrealized and we sold that business.

There was another bit of diversification that we stayed in for a short while that was profitable, but we ended up selling it anyway—filmed entertainment.

In January 1982, we announced that The Coca-Cola Company had purchased Columbia Pictures. Wall Street said we had paid too much for it and Coca-Cola stock dropped 10 percent. It looked to many people as though Roberto and I had made a substantial mistake. But in a short time the Columbia deal began to look a lot better. We had two major hits, *Tootsie* and *Gandhi*, and by the end of 1983 we posted a profit that was 50 percent higher than even our own highest expectations.

For the next several years, Columbia shored up our domestic profits and gave us excitement, and we had made the right decision to buy and operate the business. It was fun to be in the movie business, no question about it. It was very glamorous.* But as we began to grow our revenue and earnings from our rapidly expanding global soft drink business, the need for Columbia's relatively modest revenue and profit began to disappear. It was really a relatively small part of our overall business, but it was consuming an inordinate amount of time and attention. Columbia was sending a mixed message to everyone about what was really important.

In addition, the business was notoriously unpredictable. The reality of the motion picture business is that you could not develop a guaranteed stream of income from it. Herbert Allen made that clear to us from our first negotiating session and he was right. So ultimately, though our experience with movies had proved successful based on sound advice from Herbert, Roberto and I decided the company needed to return to basics.

Through Allen & Company we sold Columbia for substantially more than we paid for it.

No more mixed messages. We were not a TV company, not a movie studio. We were in the global beverage business. That was what we were best at and that

---

*We ourselves did not actually become glamorous, of course. In fact, when *Gandhi* premiered, Roberto and I were in a limousine that pulled up to the front of the theater and we were surrounded by flashing cameras. When we got out, a woman autograph seeker came rushing up, then turned away, bitterly disappointed. "Forget it," she said. "They're nobodies."

was what we wanted all of our people to be thinking about all the time.

## Another IBM Example

When John Akers was running IBM his mantra, the "new paradigm" as he called it, was to get closer to the customer than ever before, be sensitive to the customer, think like the customer.

To underline this philosophy, in early 1989 Akers convened a large meeting of IBM's key people from around the globe in Armonk, New York. It was a grand affair with lots of bells and whistles. After the opening of the meeting, Akers made a speech on the supremacy of the customer in the IBM world, and in order to highlight how important this new paradigm was, he said that as the centerpiece of this meeting I was to be the speaker at the first session.

As the morning meeting started and "before introducing Mr. Keough," Akers said more or less what follows: "I want you all to get the flavor of some of the in-depth discussions we have been carrying out here at headquarters to explore ways we can better serve our customers and reaffirm our dedication to those customers." He then showed a video of senior IBM executives, including him, with their coats off and sleeves rolled up in some clearly serious meetings on customers and customer service. There were charts and graphs and a professional facilitator who kept reminding everyone of the importance of the new paradigm.

I watched this video along with everyone else. Of course I couldn't help but notice that on the conference table in front of every executive taking part in the customer-oriented discussion was a can of Pepsi-Cola. No one said anything about it.

Then I was introduced. I thanked John for inviting me and asked if he'd do me a favor and just repeat some of that wonderful video showing IBM executives at work. At a certain point, I asked him to stop the film.

I said, "We're very proud that The Coca-Cola Company is one of the biggest customers of IBM, and you're honoring us by having me here today. Yet you put together, and I'm sure reviewed many times, this video that shows you and a number of your key executives and in front of every one of them is a can of the most competitive product my company has—Pepsi-Cola. It seems to me, John, that you could literally stop the entire meeting right now because the point has been made. You and your associates are talking about awareness of the customer, and yet as a group you are oblivious to one of your customers who is standing right here on the stage."

The audience was nervous and the oxygen left the room. Then they exploded with applause. They understood the message. Over the years that incident has become part of IBM lore.

Subsequently, IBM brought in the first outside CEO in their history, Lou Gerstner, and began to rethink just about everything. Instead of guarding their proprietary secrets, they licensed them to others. In addition, they provided information technology services to others. And under the leadership of Sam Palmisano the result is that more than half of the company's $90 billion in revenue in 2006 came from businesses that did not exist in 1990. The mixed messages were gone.

# Commandment Ten

## Be Afraid of the Future

> *"Fear is that little darkroom where*
> *negatives are developed."*
> —Michael Pritchard

MOST PEOPLE find it sensible to be prudently cautious regarding the future. It is not a crime to be cautious, but when caution becomes the overriding modus operandi in a business it can, as I've noted in Commandment One, precipitate failure. You see it all the time in football. Near the end of the game, the team with the lead begins playing it safe, cautiously protecting their lead. They quit taking the same kind of risks that gave them the lead in the first place. And all too often they lose in the final minutes of the game.

To quit taking risks is a serious risk!

But there is an even more debilitating malady lurking out there.

Fear!

There is a great difference between prudent caution regarding the future and unbridled *fear* of that future.

When FDR said that "the only thing we have to fear is fear itself," my father and mother knew exactly what he was talking about. They moved boldly ahead in the 1930s, when, truth be told, their circumstances were anything but good. But they were not going to let themselves be afraid. They had that same kind of unquenchable optimism that built this nation.

It's inspiring to me that the term the "American Dream" was coined by the historian James Truslow Adams in a book with the grand title *Epic of America*, published in 1931, when millions were out of work. He described the American Dream as "the dream of a land in which life should be better and richer and fuller for everyone." The American Dream is a resounding endorsement of the future.

Today, when that dream is more realistically attainable for more people than ever, so many look at the future and are simply afraid of it. They're not merely afraid of taking a risk. They're afraid of almost *everything*. They're afraid of life! And that is a sure recipe for failure.

We are well beyond the age when ships' captains feared disappearing into terra incognito. In the modern scientific age, in the industrialized Western world, perpetual fear of the future is irrational. But if you want to fail, it's a good posture to take.

In ancient Greek cosmology, the greatest gift the

gods possessed was the ability to know how events were going to unfold, to know the future. Mere mortal men could not do that. Not in the time of the ancient Greeks and not now.

No one knows what will happen in the days ahead. No one. Not all the soothsayers in the world or all the computer models at MIT can tell you for certain that the sun will come up tomorrow. It's possible it won't. The reality is that it probably will. But no one can know for certain.

People have always had cause to fear the unknown, but since we've become more knowledgeable, more scientifically oriented regarding the way things work, we've found there is less and less to fear in general. We feel rather certain that natural laws, such as gravity, will continue to operate with consistency. We feel fairly secure that we can sail and fly to far-off places with relative safety. We have some assurance that we can cope with quite a number of diseases that within my own memory once meant almost certain death. The TB sanitariums, the polio wards, the leper colonies have virtually disappeared. In short, we can face the future with some measure of confidence, certainly with greater confidence than when FDR implored us not to be afraid.

But we humans are contrary creatures. We have found ways to use our scientific methods to make ourselves afraid of the future in really big ways. The fact is that if there are no real fears on the horizon, we create some. With determined perversity, many among us seem to take ghoulish glee in using the most sophisticated kinds of mathematical computerized projections to forecast an imminent disaster of some kind coming at us from somewhere—everywhere. Take the little South American bee and rename it the "killer" bee. Or how about the panic over avian flu? Every newsmagazine, every newspaper, every TV anchor worried over the impending doom of large segments of the human race at the beaks of the flu-carrying birds.

In fact, while doomers and gloomers have always been with us from Jeremiah to Cassandra to Chicken Little, they have become especially persuasive since the Enlightenment, when various scientists began to apply scientific methods and statistical models to produce predictions that were not only dire, but seemed the more so because they were reinforced by what purported to be hard empirical evidence and seemingly logical thinking. It's one thing for some scraggly haired soothsayer to divine the end of the world in a cup of tea leaves. One could be skeptical. But when a man of science stands up and cites apparently irrefutable data proving a similarly catastrophic conclusion, it is difficult to argue with the data unless you have your own set of facts and figures, which not too many laymen do.

## Pessimism: Two Hundred Years of Fearmongering

Pessimism became a growth industry that really kicked into high gear with Thomas Robert Malthus, an English country parson, mathematician, and political economist. Malthus is regarded by many as the father of demography. He is most certainly the father of modern pessimism.

In *An Essay on the Principle of Population*, published in 1798, Malthus predicted that all of mankind was doomed because population would inevitably outrun food supply. He thought this would happen sometime soon, probably within the next century. The only check on this inevitable disaster was, well, *disaster* itself. Therefore, true Malthusians welcomed the Irish potato famine, which drove my ancestors to emigrate to America, as a natural correction to overpopulation. Periodic famines in India were viewed with similar benign neglect by "enlightened" Victorians who believed in the good parson's dreary math.

To this day, Malthus is the foundation and inspiration for much of the contemporary pessimism industry. In my lifetime, I've already survived the bleak prognostications of Paul R. Ehrlich, author of *The Population Bomb*. He predicted in 1968 that hundreds of millions would die of starvation in the 1970s and that life expectancy would plummet in the 1980s. It didn't happen. In 1972 the infamous Club of Rome report had us running out of all sorts of essential raw materials by the 1990s. It didn't happen. The group published a couple of *Limits-to-Growth* updates, both pretty much dead and discredited on arrival mainly because the projections assumed a static supply of resources. Human advancements in technology that find or create substitute resources were essentially ignored in these reports and human beings were viewed as if they were the same as a flock of sheep. It's true that sheep, left to their own devices, will graze in a field until all the grass is gone. *Homo sapiens* (Latin: "Man, the wise"), on the other hand, will, presumably, seek to find ways to raise more grass—or move the sheep.

Yet there is always a ready supply of despair. In raising more grass we are undoubtedly throwing some dimension of the ecosystem into imbalance, and someone will surely point it out to us. Meanwhile, to lighten the mood, turn on the TV set. There, out in the wind, wearing his yellow slicker with waves crashing just behind him is weatherman Delbert Doppler warning of a killer storm that may or may not be brewing off the Seychelles headed possibly north by northeast, or west by southwest toward the coast or out to sea. We'll keep you up to date.

> *"Worst case scenarios rarely happen."*
> —Anonymous

I'VE LIVED THROUGH the projected end of the world from global freezing in the 1970s, the near end of the world from Chernobyl in the 1980s, the even nearer end of the world from Y2K at the turn of the century, death from alar on our apples, cancer from our power lines, cancer from our cell phones, cancer from our food coloring, and cancer from the cyclamates in the diet soft drink TAB.

When the cyclamate scare hit in 1970, many in the scientific community thought the charge was baseless because such massive doses of the chemical were used. They concluded that the poor little lab rats that raised the cancer flag were getting the human equivalent of seven hundred bottles of cyclamate-sweetened soft drinks a day. It's a wonder they didn't drown. Nevertheless, cyclamates were banned and saccharin was substituted.

You would think that at some point we would grow tired of it all, that we would become aggressively pessimistic regarding the pessimism industry. But no.

**Pessimism: Focus on Failure**

Maybe, given the nature of media, it's just unavoidable. Television is the greatest gift to pessimism since Malthus himself. It is the lens through which we see the world, and it is not a flattering one.

An architect friend tells me that he can make even

the most beautiful buildings in the world look bad. All you need to do, he says, is to take a camera, use certain angles, accentuate certain features in certain ways, and virtues are made to look like flaws. Suddenly, even the most graceful skyscraper can look like an urban blight.

When you focus on the failures of the world day in and day out, it shapes your whole attitude toward life and the future. I've always liked the old couplet, attributed sometimes to Robert Louis Stevenson, sometimes just to Anonymous: "Two men looked out through prison bars. One saw mud and one saw stars." A tilt of the head, an attitude, it makes all the difference how you shape your world.

The news business has never been about good news. It's the bad stuff that makes people sit up and take notice. And that makes perfect sense. Millions of cars safely negotiating a daily commute is a nice piece of information. But ten cars in a massive pileup is *news*!

However, we've never been so inundated with news. Bad stuff is happening everywhere, all the time.

With the Internet and cable channels churning out stories 24/7, we are just up to our earlobes in warnings of disaster and reports of disaster from every corner of the globe.

Then, too, another phenomenon that multiplies our level of anxiety several times over is the *staged argument*. Increasingly, we are encouraged to believe that there are two (or more) sides to every question, even for those that can be answered with incontrovertible scientific proof. Our society, already suffering from a considerable lack of civility, is further afflicted by TV shows featuring shouting heads who pose as experts debating an issue. The conclusion you are likely to draw from such entertainments is that everything is in question, everything is up for grabs, everything has a pro and a con, and since the burden of proof is on the affirmative, the negatives usually seem to outweigh the positives in these arguments. It has always been easier to assert that the world is going to hell in a hand basket. It's always been more fun for the shouters, and more riveting, though more disturbing, for the audience.

Until the last few decades, we received our news from newspapers. No matter how lurid the headlines might be, a newspaper is a nice quiet thing. The sound of a turning page is even kind of reassuring. Radio, when it became a major source of news, still seemed more benign, much less threatening than our present TV news. Newsreels in theaters were, frankly, mostly upbeat reports of victories in World War II, or friendly features about Howard Hughes's Spruce Goose airplane or some farmer's eight-hundred-pound pumpkin.

In fact, even early television news was relatively short and fairly easy to digest. Not so now. We are bombarded into a mood of extreme despair over even the most inconsequential issues.

We are thrill seekers obsessed with safety.

There are warning signs explaining that this toaster is not a bath toy. Warning signs in hotels saying THE CALIFORNIA DEPARTMENT OF HEALTH HAS DETERMINED THAT THIS BUILDING WAS CONSTRUCTED WITH MATERIALS THAT COULD BE HAZARDOUS TO YOUR HEALTH. WELCOME TO THE MARRIOTT.

In the 2007 Wacky Warning Label Contest first prize was earned by the warning label on a small tractor: DANGER: AVOID DEATH!

Just look at children these days. It's almost as though they wear helmets to get out of bed. They are knee protected, elbow protected, car-seat enshrouded, so cocooned that they can't even look up at the sky.

In his book *State of Fear*, Michael Crichton said he was confronted with a terrible dilemma when on the same day he read that beer was a preservative of heart muscle and a carcinogen.

To top it all off, Chris Goodall, the British author of *How to Live a Low-Carbon Life* and a prominent member of the Green Party, brings us the bleak news that if we walk to the store three miles away we create more $CO_2$ than if we drive because we have to eat in order to walk and raising the food consumes so much energy that— the point is, the only solution to global warming is that we all sit in dark rooms, with the TV and refrigerator unplugged and the air-conditioning off, doing nothing and eating nothing.

## Pessimism: The Tyranny of the Past

John Bogle, founder of the Vanguard Funds, pointed out that many of us have a "rowboat" mentality. We move forward into the future the way we row a boat—facing backward, looking only at the past.

Everyone engages in a little nostalgia now and then. There's nothing like time to put a shine on even some of the most tarnished moments in history. It's human nature to remember the good and forget the bad, and we should be thankful for our memory lapses.

It's also human nature to look askance at the younger generation. Saint Augustine, Aristotle, Homer, even the ancient Assyrians, have in their time condemned young people for not respecting their elders, for being lazy, for being unruly and behaving not like people did "in the good old days."

It is alarming to read, "More than eleven-twelfths of the children in our schools do not understand the meaning of the words they read." That could have been written yesterday, but in fact it was written by Horace Mann in 1838. As Will Rogers said more than fifty years ago, "The schools are not as good as they used to be, but they never were."

A little nostalgia is harmless. Unfortunately, there are some people who truly love Bogle's rowboat and they never get past the past. The past is more or less known, more or less vaguely understood, and, therefore, for some, it is a much more comfortable place to live than the present and certainly more comfortable than the future. For such people their pessimism is truly a burden because they believe, deep down, that progress is really impossible—nothing is better than it was and nothing is going to get better. There is example after example of fear of the future leading to failure and the viruses of fear hover around business every day.

Obviously, I believe fervently in the modern philosophical idea of progress itself. We are definitely not doomed to repeat the lives of our peasant ancestors. Just look what's happened in the last century.

Around 1900 the average life expectancy in the United States was forty-seven. At that time everything we consumed was organic. The average workingman made four hundred dollars a year. We'd had a president, McKinley, assassinated in 1901. American society was then, as it always has been, in a tumultuous state. Yet people kept pouring into the country from all over the world because they truly believed that the future would be richer and fuller here.

Revolutionary changes in this country have overturned many situations that were once considered the absolute, unchangeable, and hopelessly eternal way things are. There was a time when NO IRISH NEED APPLY signs were common at employment offices. Now the Irish are everywhere.

There was a time when every door but the back door

was shut on African Americans. Gradually, these barriers are coming down. We move slowly, but gradually more and more doors have opened until today African Americans can and do legitimately aspire to the highest offices in the land.

Women once were excluded from many walks of life, including many professions and schools. Today, more than half of all college freshman classes, more than half the entrants into medical schools, law schools, and business schools are women. We move slowly, but progress is being made at even the most hidebound bastions of what some politely call "traditionalism." Or as my friend Father Ted Hesburgh at Notre Dame called it, "Reactionary pigheadedness."

In fact, my second child, Shayla, was part of the first class of women ever to go to Notre Dame. It was 1972 and Father Hesburgh made the then-revolutionary decision that Notre Dame, founded in 1842, would no longer be an all-male preserve. I remember the first day of Shayla's freshman orientation very well because there was still quite a bit of internal opposition to the whole idea, and we, the parents of the pioneer female students, not to mention the women themselves, were all a trifle nervous about how things would go.

The day began with a mass. There were these 125 young women and their families all looking on with apprehension as to how the college would treat them. Father Hesburgh, with his dramatic mane of silver hair and his white robes, strode to the altar. He had a great sense of timing and knew how critical this first moment would be to the success of the whole program. He raised his arms and looked up at the figure of the Blessed Virgin, Mary, atop the famous golden dome and said, "Mary, I want to apologize that it has taken 130 years to bring your daughters to this place."

It was an incredible moment in which we all, parents and children alike, were suffused with a glow of optimism and high hope for ourselves, for the school, and for the future of womankind in this country.

## Pessimism: The Paralysis of Fear

The late Julian Simon, the economist who wrote *The Ultimate Resource* and spent much of his career challenging the dismal notion of a Malthusian catastrophe, sounded this word of caution:

> Progress toward a more abundant material life does not come like manna from heaven. My message certainly is not one of complacency. The ultimate resource is people—especially skilled, spirited, and hopeful young people endowed with liberty—who will exert their wills and imaginations for their own benefit and inevitably benefit the rest of us as well.

Helen Keller, a woman I had the privilege of meeting many years ago, once said that "no pessimist ever discovered the secret of the stars or sailed to an uncharted land or opened a new heaven to the human spirit."

The most serious problem with great pessimism is that it is absolutely paralyzing. People are so afraid of dire consequences that they throw their hands up in despair and do nothing. Fear of the future guarantees that the future will be a failure.

Our U.S. economy has not been in a real depression since 1941, and yet in many polls large numbers of Americans are depressingly glum.

Have you noticed how often whole segments of our economy are just written off? The manufacturing sector has had its obituary written at least a dozen times by experts in the last quarter of a century. Yet as I write this, manufacturing continues to generate new and rather highly paid jobs across the country from robotics in Charleston to airplanes in Seattle. Smaller economies in the northern plains and southeast have spawned a host of new manufacturing jobs. Not to mention the entire new industries that are popping up around the urge to save energy, cut pollution, and improve the planet's environment.

Two business school professors once came to me and asked, "Based on your global experience, when is a good

time to start a new business? What are the preconditions that you look for?"

If you believe all the fearmongers, there never is a
good time to start anything. Something is always wrong.
There are always holes in the business model, always
problems lying like land mines just beneath the surface.

But if you believe in the essential creativity of entre-
preneurs, then almost any time is a good time. As to the
preconditions, simply ask: "Are there people there? Do
those people eat food and drink beverages? Is there
some kind of economic activity going on? Is there any
means of exchanging goods and services? If so, that is a
good place and a good time to start a business!"

If you are optimistic, you can afford to be patient.
Coca-Cola has, in its long history, been completely shut
out of several places for a time: all the Arab countries,
China, India, and Cuba. We are gratefully back in all of
those lands except Cuba, and the Cuban account books
are still open and I'm sure the current leadership of The
Coca-Cola Company expects to return.

*To aspire to any kind of leadership in business you sim-
ply have to be an optimist.*

That's why my association with Coca-Cola has been
such a joy. Through the Depression of the 1930s,
through World War II, through other dark times in our

nation, this product has always represented the brighter side of life. If it is nothing else, Coca-Cola is a bringer of glad tidings.

It was in that spirit that my associates and I approached our advertising in the bleak year of 1974.

What a time! President Nixon was named a co-conspirator in the infamous Watergate case and resigned in disgrace. The Mideast oil-producing countries embargoed oil shipments to the United States. Gas shortages popped up all over the country. There were bloody IRA terrorism attacks in Belfast and London, even at Harrods department store. We had our own homegrown terrorism, such as the kidnapping of Patty Hearst by some group called the Symbionese Liberation Army. India developed the atomic bomb. And we were still trying to pull out of the Vietnam War. In short, it was not a good time for America.

Therefore, it was the perfect time for Coca-Cola to be optimistic. Our marketing director, Ike Herbert, and I discussed the issue and he asked our advertising agency, creatively led at that time by Bill Backer, a remarkably talented individual, to create a theme that might help raise the sagging spirits of the country. Backer put together a wonderfully uplifting series of commercials with the title "Look Up, America."

The advertising triggered a wonderful response. People took the time to write us letters of appreciation. It demonstrated the unique role of this unique brand,

Coca-Cola, in the American psyche. Coca-Cola had an ability, in a small way, to influence the national mood. With that ability came responsibility. It was the responsibility to never do anything in our marketing that was in bad taste. We had an obligation to consistently demonstrate our faith in the future.

*To aspire to any kind of leadership in business you simply have to be a rational optimist.*

One optimist in a sea of pessimists can make all the difference.

Aristotle contended in his treatise De Anima in the fourth century B.C. that there are five senses: sight, smell, hearing, taste, and touch. There has been agreement on that number ever since. I believe there is, however, a sixth: the ability to sense a mood. Call it intuition or insight or sensitivity, whatever you want to call it, those who are successful have it. Great marketers have it. Great political and business leaders have it.

They know what the prevailing mood is and, when it is negative, they sense how to change it.

Some years ago, the Coca-Cola bottling business in the Philippines, which had always been a strong business since the end of the Spanish-American War, began a downward spiral. It was controlled by a local company called San Miguel, whose leaders wanted to concentrate on expanding their beer business and began to ignore its soft drink base. By 1981, the tide had turned badly and Pepsi was outselling Coke two to one in the Philippines.

Eventually, the owners of San Miguel were persuaded by John Hunter, one of our top executives, to allow us to run the Coca-Cola bottling operation under a joint operating agreement.

The equipment remained the same. The twelve thousand employees remained the same. We just changed two things. John Hunter, an Australian who had worked for Coca-Cola in Japan and the Pacific Rim, took over the region for The Coca-Cola Company and Neville Isdell, an Irishman who had worked in South Africa with Coca-Cola and briefly in Australia, took over the bottling operations and the twelve thousand employees became his team.

John and Neville worked together to change and energize the Philippine bottling company. Neville reinvigorated the several thousand bottling company employees and a plan was developed and executed. There were political problems in the Philippines that added a level of stress for everyone. Then, too, the competition had become very aggressive in their tactics and pricing. But above all else, Neville, as head of the bottling operations, listened and realized that the employees had a very low opinion of themselves and a very pessimistic, even fearful, view of their future. The business was basically what it had always been. The mood, though, was gloomy.

Neville even put on fatigues and led pep rallies. He constantly walked through the plant, greeting people by name, asking about their families. He rode out on trucks to make deliveries and talk with customers. He had this contagious kind of enthusiasm that defies quantifying, but you know it when you see it. It's leadership.

In one year, two people, Hunter and Isdell, working together, highly focused, turned the results around completely. Coca-Cola was outselling Pepsi two to one.

What had Neville Isdell done with bottling company employees? He connected with his people and basically convinced them that they were better than the competition. He also gave them a bright picture of the future. He was passionate in his optimism and that rubbed off on everyone from the lowliest sweeper to the highest volume customer in Manila.

John Hunter went on to become executive vice president of The Coca-Cola Company in charge of international operations and on retirement from the company became chairman of the international operations of Seagram's.

Neville led our operations in Europe and became chairman of one of our largest bottling companies, and, as I write this book, he is chief executive officer of The

Coca-Cola Company and still exudes that contagious optimism.

The pessimists tell us the world was born in chaos and has been going downhill ever since. But we have to live with some hope. We have to live with some faith in our fellow men. We have to act as if there will be a tomorrow, there is some point in starting an enterprise, in starting a family, in admiring the sunset, in going on.

If you want to fail, be afraid of the future. If you want to succeed, approach the future with optimism—and passion.

And that brings me to a little added bonus—an eleventh commandment.

## Commandment Eleven

# Lose Your Passion for Work—
# for Life

> *"Nothing great in the world
> has been accomplished without passion."*
> —Georg Wilhelm Friedrich Hegel

MY FATHER ONCE SAID that the genius of this country is contained in a few words in our Declaration of Independence: "Life, Liberty, and the pursuit of Happiness." The latter phrase was intriguing to him. It said that the Founding Fathers believed there should be more to life than just struggle. There should be bread, but roses too.

Being Irish he had certainly had his share of exposure to the dark and keening side of existence, so he was doubly impressed by his nation that was born with the audacity—the incredible optimism—to include that word "happiness" right there in its foundation principles.

"Happiness!" No one really knows what it is, but this country was founded on the conviction that it could be attained.

I have my own view of what happiness is in the context of a business career.

The old saying "Tell me what you love and I'll tell you who you are" is true. Love has been around a long time. The word comes from the ancient Vedic, or Hindu, word of the Sanskrit "lubh," meaning desire. A major component of happiness in the business world is finding something you love doing, whatever it might be, and then finding a way to do it. To have success you have to have a high level of unadulterated desire to get up and go to work.

Warren Buffett says, "I tap-dance to work every day." That has been my philosophy as well.

It's not that work has to be fun. That's a misconception promoted by some of the more giddy human resources people who like to talk about team spirit and sing "Kumbaya." Work, real work, is often very hard, exhausting at times. Rallying the troops (as Neville Isdell did in the Philippines) is not telling people to have more fun. It's telling them to work harder because they are capable of doing better. They deserve, for their own self-satisfaction, to perform at a higher level. The hard work itself is what takes you tap-dancing into the office. It's that passion to solve the problems of the day.

If you really want to fail, lose that passion for whatever it is you're doing. Get that spring out of your step. Say to yourself, "That's good enough." Or "That's not my job." Or "I don't care." Or "I'm retiring soon anyway."

We all know people who have done this. They are the gray-faced automatons found in every workplace— the people who seem to stew in their own misery, cursing the darkness rather than lighting a candle. We all know them, and they are failures. Even if they manage to make a good living, they are failures because they have set such low expectations for themselves and everyone around them.

I have never met a successful person who did not express love for what he did and care about it passionately. I have never met a business leader or a political leader or a journalist or an artist or teacher or doctor, or anyone, who is really great at what he or she does who does not display a genuine passion for that work—so much so that if you ask them they'll tell you they can't imagine doing anything else. They seem almost a little crazy about it.

I know that in this age of careers that can span many jobs at many different companies the notion of passion seems antiquated. How can you be passionate about anything that is going to last only a few years, and then you're going to move on to something else? What's the point?

All the more reason why you have to be passionate.

At the outset I said that I had no surefire how-to formulas for success. And I don't. But I do have a couple of bits of advice on how to develop passion for your job. I strongly believe it can be cultivated.

Shakespeare wrote, "All the world's a stage."

In his influential sociological work, *The Presentation of Self in Everyday Life*, Erving Goffman elaborated on Shakespeare's observation, noting that whatever we do, we all have to be *performers*, in one way or another—and often in several changing roles. The store clerk performs for her customers. The waiter performs for his patrons. The lawyer performs for his clients, for the court, and/or for his associates. The doctor performs for his patients and/or for his associates. The executive performs for his employees and/or his superiors.

To succeed in our various performances we have to strive to make an emotional connection with the audience, whoever that audience might be in a particular setting. You have to create, within yourself, an intense emotional drive for what you are doing at the time you are doing it. See yourself in your role. Understand what your role is at that moment.

In high school I was complaining about a boring subject. My mother said, "Donald, there is no such thing as a boring subject. What's boring is your refusal to try to find what makes it interesting."

Throughout my life, in many different situations in

many different countries I've consciously worked to become interested in the immediate moment and make an emotional connection with the people involved. I've consciously tried to block out peripheral issues and noise and listen intently to the person I'd be dealing with— and find what makes his or her particular concern interesting. In just a few seconds I'd find that I could share their interest.

There have been many distasteful situations when I wished that I didn't have to do a particular task that was facing me. But I would look at the situation and consciously think to myself, "What good can come out of this? What is the redeeming feature here? What is my role to bring it about?" And I've generally found something good because I was determined to do so. Even having to fire someone, which is probably the worst task one can face, I looked for ways to guide the person toward a more fruitful career or a more suitable company.

You have to be passionate about doing the job at hand to get the best results possible. The easiest way to develop an inner passion in a business setting is to focus all your mind and heart on four aspects of your world: your customers, your brands, your people, and, finally, your dreams.

## Make an Emotional Connection
## with Your Customers

Remind yourself every day as to just what the customer is looking for, expects, wants from your company. Is it a product? Is it a service? Is it an experience? Is it help, care, advice, expertise? Maybe it's all of these. Maybe it's different things for different customers. But constantly do your best to think like those people out there who are going to pay you for providing or doing something. It is so easy to lose sight of the customer, to think dispassionately about an amorphous mass called the market or a market segment.

There are, except as statistical abstractions, no such things as market segments. There are only people. They have faces. Visualize your audience. Visualize specific people and think hard about just what you're going to do for them that day. For years I had a photograph in my office depicting a woman in her thirties pushing a loaded shopping cart while holding on to a crying three-year-old and with an anguished look on her face. The caption read "This is your consumer."

With the Coca-Cola Foods Division and later with The Coca-Cola Company itself, I would often stop at a supermarket or a fast-food outlet and just listen to shoppers or patrons. Ad agencies would describe prototypical customers for us, giving us lots of statistical data on their preferences and their lifestyles. But from time to time I just needed to hear their voices. I just found it necessary to develop some emotional connection, some passionate attachment to those I wanted to serve. I wanted to care about that lady, that man, that family. I genuinely wanted them to have a pleasant experience with our products.

## Make an Emotional Connection with Your Brands

I fell in love with everything I ever sold. Next to Mickie, my children, and grandchildren, the most passionate relationship of my life involved the brands I was privileged to represent. It was Coca-Cola for decades and today it's the Allen brand and Allen & Company.

And while I was not always successful, I wanted to further protect, strengthen, and enhance them. If they were new brands, I wanted to nurture them and build a strong platform for them.

A brand or a brand name is the most powerful force in business. Without it, you're just dealing in commodities and anyone can come along and carve out a share of your business. But with a good brand you have a weapon to defend your business and a foundation on which to build the future. If you're selling tissue, you're just selling something that lots of people sell. But if you sell Kleenex, you have something special to offer.

There just is no substitute for the solid brand. This is driven home again and again in so many ways. In 2007, the power of the brand was demonstrated once more in a study run by Stanford. Ordinary and identical foods—milk, apple juice, and carrots—were given to individuals in separate packages. One package was wrapped in plain paper. The other was wrapped in the familiar McDonald's golden arches package.

You, of course, could have anticipated the results. No matter what the food was, the individuals preferred the McDonald's package. Even the carrots tasted better to them.

A brand is magic and it will thrive when it is in the hands of those who understand its magic and treat it with passionate care. A law firm becomes a brand. A hospital becomes a brand, and in a very real sense, the U.S.A. is a brand. Treated with love, a brand will stir passion among consumers, and, I might add, investors.

Treated badly, like Schlitz beer was, the brand and perhaps the whole company will just disappear.

## Make an Emotional Connection with Your People

It is said by many companies, "People are our most important asset."

I've been fortunate to be a part of companies that actually took the wisdom of this cliché to heart. My current corporate home, Allen & Company, has a unique culture that, as Herbert Allen once described it, is "a welfare state for employees, and raw capitalism for the principals." Under his highly effective management philosophy, staff employees are generously salaried and they often receive rich bonuses that in great years match their pay. Managing directors, however, have no safety nets. They earn a percentage of only the business that they are able to generate. This arrangement might not work well in all firms, but it seems to satisfy everyone at Allen & Company, and the loyalty rate reflects that fact. The Allen culture treats people as if they were truly our most important asset because they simply are.

Based on the evidence, however, not too many companies actually believe that. If they did, they would all make the *Fortune* list of best places to work, and they wouldn't find their top talent drifting off to other firms.

I've mentioned one reason why people may leave a company—the bureaucracy stifles them.

Another reason they leave is that they simply don't have anything to be passionate about. Towers Perrin, a recruiter, conducted a survey and found that more than 35 percent of employees worldwide described themselves as disengaged and disenchanted.

For good employees, while money and power are important, even more important is the opportunity to be a part of something that kindles a passionate fire of enthusiasm. There simply is no greater motivation than giving an employee a challenge that demands a deep, passionate involvement, requiring their best effort.

In 1907 Ernest Shackleton was trying to raise a crew to sail with him on his exploration of the South Pole. He took out an ad in the London *Times* that read: "Wanted. Men for hazardous journey. Low wages. Bitter cold. Long hours of complete darkness. Safe return doubtful. Honor and recognition in the event of success." The next morning, so the story goes, more than five thousand men lined up outside the newspaper's office hoping to be one of the few selected for the trip.

Most people have a strong desire—a passion—to achieve something worthwhile, even when the odds are against them. Give them a significant piece of the puzzle and they will try to solve it for you. In any business, if a worthwhile challenge is given to employees and presented with passionate enthusiasm and if they are shown how their own passionate dedication and talent can be applied to meet that challenge, in my experience a vital sense of excitement will flow like electricity throughout the business.

Passion in one area sparks passion in other areas. It is contagious and leads to new ideas and new energy.

## Make an Emotional Connection
## with Your Dreams

Dreams do not come true by wishing, but if you internalize them and determine to grow into them and visualize them coming true, then there is a greater chance that they will be realized. We are all in what Teilhard de Chardin calls a state of "becoming." He wrote about striving to reach the omega point, where the forces coalesce in our lives and we reach as close to perfection as we can. One always falls short, but it is the striving that counts.

Someday you will not be doing what you're doing now. Think about your corner of the world at the moment, and think about how you'd like it to look when you move on.

Many people spend all their years and never learn this valuable lesson—there is more to life than having everything. As you go through your working life, in every job you do, decide that this is the last job you will ever have and, therefore, whatever the assignment determine you want to leave it better than you found it.

The Ten Commandments for Business Failure all come with my personal guarantee that if you follow them steadfastly and consistently, you will fail.

But Commandment Eleven is the most important of them all because passion is essential to continue and expand the American Dream. I have had the benefits of that dream all my life, and I hope that others will for generations to come.

Optimism and passion are the warp and the woof of the same fabric of leadership and social progress.

If you want to fail, you can ignore these psychological factors.

But if you want to succeed, then apply them to turning your corner of the world into a better place.

A word of caution: Don't be afraid of the criticism that great enthusiasm and optimism sometimes engender among the cynical, the "realists."

"Be realistic" is appropriate advice in some instances, but before you leap to accept it, ask yourself if being realistic is not just an easy way to discard a higher, more idealistic goal—a vision of something extraordinary perhaps that others around you do not yet see or understand.

> *"The reasonable man adapts himself to the world. The unreasonable man persists in trying to adapt the world to himself. All progress, therefore, depends upon the unreasonable man."*
> —George Bernard Shaw

THIS PLANET OF OURS with its more than six billion fallible human beings and with all its tragic flaws is still a marvelous place. Wherever one looks there is something that could stand a bit of improving. While many would argue, I've always believed that business is one of the key instruments for improving the opportunity for people around the globe. I've always believed that serving in the business community is more than a privilege. With it comes the responsibility to make things better than they are. In my fortunate life in the Coca-Cola business, I've seen vivid examples of that in every corner of the world.

Some sixteen hundred years ago Saint Augustine wrote: "Hope has two beautiful daughters. Their names are Anger and Courage. Anger that things are the way they are. Courage to make them the way they ought to be."

If you want a better world for your children and grandchildren, believe! Believe that one individual can make a difference. And that individual can be you.

You will fail if you quit taking risks, are inflexible, isolated, assume infallibility, play the game close to the line, don't take time to think, put all your faith in outside experts, love your bureaucracy, send mixed messages, and fear the future.

On the bright side, there is redemption. React in time, recognize the danger signs, and you can probably extricate yourself from one or even more of these traps. It's hard for people and companies to avoid them sometimes. As I've confessed, the leaders of The Coca-Cola

Company, including me, have been guilty of some of these failings from time to time. But never for very long. That's the way it is with great companies and smart people. No matter what happens they are never mired in failure. They fall but always find ways to pick themselves up and move on.

> *"They laughed at Joan of Arc,*
> *but she went right ahead and built it anyway."*
> —Gracie Allen

# Acknowledgments

No BOOK, even a little one, is a one-man effort. During the past twenty-five years I've had the privilege of being associated with two people who have helped me clarify and shape my spoken and written communications. As I have found myself communicating verbally with an ever-widening circle of individuals, John White has worked with me as my executive assistant and partner since 1981. He is an expert in the written word and has superb judgment. He has been a sounding board and editor through all those years.

David Blomquist, a true renaissance man, has had to suffer over these years by often taking my thoughts and ideas and helping to rationalize and organize them. David has challenged me when my thinking was vague and unclear and in the process helped shape my written and spoken words into messages appropriate for every audience.

Niall O'Dowd, the cofounder and publisher of *Irish American Magazine* and the *Irish Voice* and recognized as an important player in the Northern Ireland peace process, has been a confidant. With a typical journalist's exploration, he has discovered a great deal about my heritage, which has found its way into this book and other publications.

This little book would certainly have remained unpublished had it not been for the courageous determination of Adrian Zackheim, founder and publisher of Portfolio. Courtney Young, my editor, raised cogent and thoughtful questions and offered suggestions that greatly improved the quality of the manuscript.

Alfred Lord Tennyson in *Ulysses* observed that "I am a part of all that I have met" and that is especially true in my case. My early years, obviously, were greatly influenced by my mother, Veronica, and father, Leo. My mother, who loved music and painting, instilled in me a love of the arts and literature. My father, who suffered through a series of family setbacks, was always passionate about the future, achieved his business goals, and put integrity as the number-one measure of a well-spent life.

Through the years, I have been blessed to know and work with and for an amazing collection of individuals: among them, Paul Gallagher of Paxton and Gallagher, Clarke and Gilbert Swanson, Charles Duncan, Luke Smith, Paul Austin, Roberto Goizueta, Herbert Allen, Barry Diller, Jack Welch, and Jimmy Williams.

Robert W. Woodruff, patriarch of The Coca-Cola Company, welcomed me into the Coca-Cola family and I enjoyed the great privilege of spending time with him in the later years of his life.

Warren Buffett and I first met each other in 1960, when I bought a house across the street from him in Omaha. Our long, close relationship is a book in itself. I count it a great honor to serve on the board of Berkshire Hathaway. What is there to say about Warren that the world does not know? Well, I can say he is a dear friend and a wonderful human being who is at the top of his game. He is the world's greatest simplifier. Take complex economic theories or business problems and in a biblical way, he makes easily understood parables out of them. He is everyone's hero, including mine.

I retired from The Coca-Cola Company on April 14, 1993. The next day Herbert Allen asked me to become nonexecutive chairman of Allen & Company. Herbert in a very real sense is the most remarkable man I ever met. He is a special combination of wit and wisdom, generous to a fault, interested in the major issues that confront our society, and a closet intellectual. When I joined Allen & Company, he probably thought I'd serve for a year or two. Fourteen years later I'm still here. He's stuck with me. My title is grand, my responsibilities are less than modest, and I'm having the time of my life as part of this family-run firm. It's exciting to be Herbert's friend and business partner and to work with his sons and a cadre of remarkable associates.

Every now and then you cross paths with an individual who makes an enormous personal impact on you. For me that person is Father Ted Hesburgh, the ninety-year-old president emeritus of the University of Notre Dame. Father Ted is a multidimensional person: priest, educator, public servant, confidant to six presidents, a three-time special ambassador, thirty-five years as president of Notre Dame, the past chairman of overseers at Harvard, and an individual with the most honorary degrees in history. *Time* magazine called him one of the most respected persons in America. Father Ted has been a cherished friend and counselor to me and my family.

Finally, there is the joy of having shared a remarkable life journey of more than fifty years with my wife, Mickie. Our six children, their six spouses, and eighteen grandchildren have brought and continue to bring great pleasure into our lives. All in all it's truly been a wonderful life . . . so far.